Runnin' Around

The Serving House Book of Infidelity

Runnin' Around

The Serving House Book of Infidelity

Edited by
Thomas E. Kennedy and Walter Cummins

SERVING HOUSE BOOKS

Contents

Open a Secret Door

This collection grew from our immediate reaction to reading Stephen Dunn's poem "The Imagined" in the March 14, 2011 issue of *The New Yorker*. We decided the world would both welcome and need a work subtitled *The Serving House Book of Infidelity*. After all, we had published *The Serving House Book of Worst Meals*.

Since addressing the taste buds, it was time to turn to other appetites. Would the result be a suppressant or a stimulus? We wouldn't know until we invited a group of poets and writers to contribute and saw what turned up. Many were enthusiastic in accepting the challenge, especially when we assured people their submissions needn't be personal admissions or confessions, but they could be.

Though the usual connotation of infidelity is sexual—as typified by Mark Hillringhouse's cover photo with its overt signage for day-rate clandestine encounters—infidelity can take many forms. People can lust in their hearts as well as on rumpled sheets. They can be unfaithful to a value or a memory or a promise. But illicit sex does get our attention, as seen in many thousand hours of soap operas and decades of movies, not to mention *Madame Bovary* and *Anna Karenina*.

With Stephen Dunn's kind permission, his poem leads off this gathering of poems, stories, and essays. The wit and insight of "The Imagined" reveal the source behind most infidelity, the fantasy of something more alluring and exciting than the lives we live, often carnal delights with an idealized partner, one of flawless sensuality. Advertising overwhelms us with the possibilities, a world that's a version of Garrison Keillor's Lake Wobegon, where—in this case—all the men and women are stunningly attractive (and multi-orgasmic to boot) and eager to slip into our lives through that secret doorway.

While that door may open to erotic dreams, in the cold light of day it may just be the entrance to a rundown day-rate motel room with peeling paint and stains that make you shiver.

Clearly, a group of talented authors has much to say about the subject. Let's see how our contributors explore infidelity. We hereby invite you into the world and our pages of infidelity.

Walter Cummins
Thomas E. Kennedy

Stephen Dunn

THE IMAGINED

If the imagined woman makes the real woman
seem bare-boned, hardly existent, lacking in
gracefulness and intellect and pulchritude,
and if you come to realize the imagined woman
can only satisfy your imagination, whereas
the real woman with all her limitations
can often make you feel good, how, in spite
of knowing this, does the imagined woman
keep getting into your bedroom, and joining you
at dinner, why is it that you always bring her along
on vacations when the real woman is shopping,
or figuring the best way to the museum?

And if the real woman

has an imagined man, as she must, someone
probably with her at this very moment, in fact
doing and saying everything she's ever wanted,
would you want to know that he slips in
to her life every day from a secret doorway
she's made for him, that he's present even when
you're eating your omelette at breakfast,
or do you prefer how she goes about the house
as she does, as if there were just the two of you?
Isn't her silence, finally, loving? And yours
not entirely self-serving?   Hasn't the time come,

once again, not to talk about it?

Timmy Waldron

All My Lovers Were Liars, Too

The water had a bad chop to it from the wind and the boat fell with a slap over every swelling whitecap. Each time I tried to drink I ended up spilling beer on my shirt or knocking the aluminum can into my front teeth. The Golden Gate Bridge, shrinking behind us, looked like an easily breakable model from a Godzilla movie set. I tried to light a cigarette a few times, but the wind and our speed made it just as impossible as drinking. It was late afternoon, but still bright from the sinking sun above and the reflection shining up from the surface of the bay below. Once we were a little past Alcatraz, Bobby cut the engine. Me, him, and JB lit smokes. Bobby lifted a vial of coke from his pocket and tossed it to JB. The boat rose and sank with the swells. I could feel the drop in the pit of my stomach. JB took a bump and handed it off to me. I hit it and gave it back to Bobby. He used this apparatus he called *The Bullet*. It had a built-in glass straw that filled up with coke when you turned it over. You could take a bump without having to dump the coke out and snort it from another surface. We lit another round of smokes.

I didn't like Bobby all that much, and I'm pretty sure he didn't care for me. He was interested in a girl me and JB knew and was being nice to us because of that. He paid for our drinks when we saw him out, and even bought us dinner once. This boat trip was part of his plan to win us over, or at least to get us to owe him something. Barry Bonds was on his way to smashing the all-time home run record for a season and Bobby offered to take us to the park so we could watch the record breaking run fly into the bay with our own eyes.

JB sunk into the starboard seat. He was staring at me and I tried not to notice. We'd known each other since high school, a decade of friendship at that point. We'd also been roommates for two years by then. It was obvious that something was wrong with him. He didn't look good, like he hadn't been sleeping much. Lately all of our minor exchanges at the house were elusively uncomfortable. Normally I'd ask him what was wrong, but I had been sleeping with his girlfriend on and off for some time. I was afraid he had caught on.

JB introduced me and Martha a few years back and we went out a couple of times. JB and her both went to the same college and they had a bit of history together. As JB told it, "Almost every time I cheated on my girlfriend, I did it with Martha." For whatever reason Martha and I didn't work out and she started seeing JB. It didn't take more than a few dates before they let it be known that they were boyfriend and girlfriend. I told myself that it didn't bother me, stuff like that had happened between me and him a bunch of times over the years. We dated the same girls on and off in high school. On more than one occasion we stepped over one another to get with this one or that one. But there was something about what happened with Martha that nagged at me. I tried to set aside the feeling as best I could and eventually it was so muted that I didn't think it was an issue. A big part of that was Zelda. Martha introduced me to her. She was another college friend that moved out to San Francisco after graduation. We hit it off pretty good and started dating. We were all doing these jobs that we kind of just fell into and there was a weird feeling like these jobs were pretend and our lives outside of work were more real and that this was kind of killing time before life started and everything became awesome all the time. I think we felt famous. And for no other reason than we were young and hadn't been disappointed enough, yet.

Me and Zelda dated for awhile and fell into a real good relationship. It was nice and easy and I wasn't anxious or stressed all the time. In those ways it was better than any relationship I'd ever had before. We had similar interests, drinking, fucking, and watching TV. I eventually messed up our good run. We were day drinking on a Sunday at Joxer Daly's Pub in West Portal. Before dark we headed back to my place to fool around. I was sitting up in the bed and she was lying in my arms looking up at me, I gave her a kiss and said, "You're dying to marry me." I was kidding. I liked to tease her sometimes and she liked it too, but sometimes I'd go too far and upset her. We had never talked about marriage before and I was too dumb to realize how serious she'd take it.

"Yes," she said. "I would love to marry you." Her cheeks went red and she turned her face into my lap to hide her embarrassment. That night, when we fucked, I told her I never wanted to fuck anyone other than her for the rest of my life. She lit up like I'd never seen, before. The next morning was awkward. Zelda told me how much fun she had and how happy she was. I told her I had a great time, but had trouble remembering leaving the bar and asked her how we got home.

"You drink too much," she said as she dressed. Zelda was a red head with fair skin. She always looked amazing when she was angry. I shrugged, and then she left.

There were so many boats in McCovey Cove that we couldn't get anywhere close. It didn't matter. We were high and going to be drunk and it was an exciting place to be. I wasn't even a Giants fan. Bobby eased the boat into the crowd and dropped anchor. He opened the cooler and passed around beers, then tuned in the pre-game show on the radio. JB was still staring me down. He caught himself doing it and changed his demeanor, but it kept getting uncomfortable. In a strange unselfish moment, Bobby asked JB how Martha was.

"Good," he said. "She's home in Chicago for the week."

"Oh, shit, I bet you'll be up to no good," Bobby said. He drank some beer and then turned to me, "And how about Zelda?"

"She's good," I said and shrugged. JB rolled his eyes. "We're talking about getting married."

"To each other?" JB asked.

"Yeah," I told him. JB's posture changed completely. He straightened his backbone and sat up like this was the greatest news he'd ever heard. "I mean we're not engaged, yet. We just talked about it."

"But you want to get married?" JB asked, "To her?"

"I don't know," I said. "I think I do."

"Congrats, man." Bobby gave me a bear hug and lifted me off my feet. The movement of the boat caused him to lose his footing and we fell into JB and I knocked my head into his pretty good. We cursed and then laughed it off. After that, we were pretty happy. We drank and smoked and did some more coke. It was good to hang out with JB like this again. It seemed like we hadn't really enjoyed each other's company for some time. Bobby had kept his ulterior motive to himself as long as the coke and beer would let him and then started talking non-stop about Kelly. Me and JB both knew she wasn't interested in Bobby, but we listened to him talk while we waited for the game to start. We turned up the radio as a hint and got him to quiet down for the first few innings, but the worse the Giants played the less Bobby paid attention to the game and the more he brought up Kelly. Even though the Dodgers were pretty much in control of the game the whole time, it seemed like the Giants had a chance to overtake them, and secure a spot in the playoffs. Bobby swore up and down that he'd get us tickets if they made it. He also made us promise to help him hook-up with Kelly, again and again.

Bonds knocked out his record breaking home runs seventy-one and seventy-two, neither ball made it to the water, the Giants lost. It wouldn't have mattered even if he hit them out of the park. It was a night game and none of us were dressed warm enough for the weather on the bay. We left at the bottom of the sixth and didn't hear about what happened until we got back to the docks. Bobby invited me and JB out for more drinks, he said he'd buy. It was a Friday and he wanted to keep hanging out. We didn't even bother to come up with an excuse and just told him no. We took the Muni back to West Portal and opted to stop for a few drinks at Joxer's. We talked shit about Bobby the whole ride back. Ganging up on him always brought the two of us closer together.

The first time I had seen Zelda after she stormed out was fine, at first. We met at a bar in North Beach near all the strip clubs and Italian restaurants. We talked and drank and laughed and I thought the marriage thing was forgotten. When we got back to my place, back in bed, it was like we were right back in that moment.

"Are you going to remember this?" She asked me.

"I'm not that drunk."

"How do you know?" She asked. "You could be blacked out, right now."

"I'm not that bad," I said. "Not even close."

"Sometimes when you drink you get this look in your eyes, like you're not even there." She adjusted under the sheets, took her panties off, and threw them onto the sofa chair where she kept her clothes in a pile when she stayed over. She left the ripped and faded *Nevermind* t-shirt that she had stolen from me on as a nighty. "You get these shark eyes. It freaks me out."

"Doll's eyes," I said, doing my best imitation of Quint from the movie *Jaws*. She made a face as I leaned in and kissed her. She tried to squirm away, like we weren't done talking, but I pulled her close and kissed her harder. Once she relaxed, I let go and slid my hand under the covers and in between her legs. I started to finger her. She moaned and moved a little bit, then she found my rhythm and her hips began to move and collided with my hand. I was hard. We fucked and then slept and didn't talk any more about marriage that night. The next morning she was awake before me, just sitting up in the bed. I opened my eyes.

"Are we getting married or what?" She asked.

JB bought the first round at Joxer's. We knocked our pints together and cheered each other. It was a bit past eleven at night and the bar was busy. We drank there a lot and over tipped all the time, so we never had a problem getting drinks. Before the first beer was gone it was apparent that throwing Bobby under the bus had lost its appeal.

"Where's Zelda tonight," JB asked.

"Working," I said. She was a nanny and worked for a wealthy couple that paid well and let her live in the apartment over their detached garage, over in Sunset. Zelda liked the job, she said the little guy she took care of was great to be around and her bosses were easy to get along with. The only catch was that they loved to go out on Friday and Saturday nights, so we rarely got together before Sunday.

"I should call Martha," he said.

"Tell her I said hi," I said. JB gave me a sour smile and walked outside the bar.

Martha had called me at work. This was the week after Zelda had confronted me about the marriage proposal. She had something she wanted to talk to me about and asked if I could meet her for lunch.

"Don't tell JB," she said before hanging up on me. It was strange, but not that strange. Me and Martha spent a lot of time together, but it was always with JB and Zelda. I figured she was planning something for JB's birthday or something. We met at an empty restaurant by the bay and had oysters with a lemon shallot sauce and bottle of white wine that she said was good for the price.

"Is JB cheating on me?" she asked, interrupting something I was saying that didn't really matter too much.

"Why would you ask me that?"

"I've got a feeling he's cheating on me," she said. "But I also think I might be acting crazy."

"I know what you mean." I poured the last bit of wine into my glass and thought about how much I didn't want to go back to work. "Sometimes I get the feeling that Zelda has this whole life going on that I know nothing about."

"Well," she said. "Is he?" I shook my head and thought about how a few months back we were out and this girl was talking to me and I was flirting with her and JB jumped in and swooped her away from me. I knew I wasn't going to sleep with her, but I liked the attention and he couldn't stand to let me have it. He went back to her place and I went home. In the morning he kicked open my door and threw her soiled thong in my face and laughed. I laughed too, like it was the most awesome thing ever, but it wasn't. I hated it.

"I don't know," I said, nodding my head up and down.

"Don't lie to protect your friend," she said.

"It's not like that," I told her. "Let's get some more wine."

"I'm broke."

"Me too."

"I've got a few bottles at my place" she said. "Left over from the party."

I called my boss from a pay phone and told her that I ate some bad oysters and was having sharp intestinal pains. JB and I had come to the conclusion that saying you had diarrhea was the best way to call out of work. It was so embarrassing that the person you were lying to would most likely believe you. At the very least they would be too embarrassed to challenge you. I made sure Martha was out of ear shot when I made the call. My boss said fine and hung up on me. Most days I'd feel guilty about ditching out on work, but on that day I was already lost in wine-fueled daydreams of what would happen back at Martha's place.

I started to get nervous as soon as we got on the Muni. We took the M from Embarcadero and switched to the N at Van Ness and got off at Cole. I kept wiping my brow with my sleeve to stop the sweat from beading up on my forehead. We got to her house and I plopped down on the futon while she opened the wine. Martha handed me a giant glass, filled to the brim with some cheap California white, and sat down next to me. We talked and drank for a little while without bringing up JB or Zelda.

"I think JB lies to me about where he is and who he's with," Martha finally said. She sounded sad and broken, not as anxious as she did in the restaurant.

"Zelda lies to me, too," I said and then we started kissing.

I had convinced Martha to get an abortion. I had imagined it was going to be a long difficult conversation between me and her, but it barely took a minute. I think she just wanted someone else to say it first. I told her that I'd be with her after, to take care of her. She was too afraid that it would be suspicious, both of us being out of town on the same weekend. Zelda and JB would both have to know we were gone at the same time and even if they didn't think we were running away together, they'd have to say something, even if they were joking. She decided to go home to Chicago and have it done. She had close friends that still lived there and they would take care of her after.

"She's not picking up," JB said after returning from outside.

"She's probably just out with friends or whatever."

"I don't know." He took a sip from his pint and shook his head. "She's been acting weird lately."

"Girls are weird."

"No," he said. "Like cagey or something."

"I'm sure it's all in your head."

"You didn't tell her I fucked that girl did you?"

"Which one?"

"Fuck you." He downed the rest of his beer. "Get the next round." He flashed a baggy of coke that he must have swiped from Bobby and then tucked it back into his jeans. "I'm going to load up two smokes. Meet you out front."

When we had coke we'd pack our cigarettes as much as we could. We'd slam the pack against our palms for minutes at a time to hollow out the tip of the cigarette. I didn't bother doing it that day and I guess JB knew that, so he went into the john and stuck the cigarettes into the baggy and sucked the coke into them like a straw. I wasn't outside too long, before he met me and handed me one. I looked at the tip of the cigarette, full of white powder, and nodded my thanks to him. I handed him a road soda that I picked up inside and took a sip of my own. At Joxer's, before they got fined for doing this, they would give you beer in a Styrofoam cup and let you drink it while you smoked out front. There were a couple other people smoking, but we lit up anyway. When you freebase through a cigarette it doesn't really smell noticeably. I smoked the cigarette in a couple big drags and then gulped down half of my road soda. The world had changed.

"Fight," JB said to me. He pointed up the street to two guys throwing wild punches at each other in the street.

"Let's go check it out," I said. We started walking up West Portal towards the Muni tunnel where the street came to a T, that's where the guys were fighting. They were swinging at each other without aim or control. Every punch was a well-telegraphed haymaker, which often missed or landed sloppily. The pair was moving all over the place. One would throw a volley of swings, backing the other across the street, and then the other would hold his ground and push the other back and start to retaliate. There was hardly any sound, no Indiana Jones exploding thuds when they connected. Just the shuffling of feet and maybe something that sounded like the slap of meat. As we got closer to the fight we could see a crowd outside of the Philosopher's Club, the Italian bar in West Portal. We drank there sometimes, it had a nice long bar, and Golden Tee in the back. The bartender was an ex-marine who fought in Granada and saw his best friend gutted right in front of him, if you believe him at his word. He always had rowdy friends in the Phi-Lo Club, drinking, other ex-marines, I guessed.

"Fight must have started in the Phi-Lo Club," JB said.

"I don't think we should get any closer," I said. "Those guys are kind of all over the place." The brawl came right at us. I took a few steps back, but JB held his ground. The guy being pushed towards us was bald. His white tee shirt was stretched out around the collar from being pulled on and grabbed at by his opponent with crew-cut black hair. I could hear their grunts and strains as they swatted at each other. Mumbled curses punctuated their deep breaths. The bald man made a stand at the curb and pushed the guy with the crew cut back with both hands and then started his charge. I heard laughter come from the group of onlookers outside the Phi-Lo. I don't know if they were laughing at the fight or me for flinching. I was embarrassed just the same.

The fight made it to the other side of the intersection. By then, the Phi-Lo patrons had had enough. They circled the two brawlers and broke them apart. In short order the fight was over and the group was filing back into their bar.

We walked back to Joxer's and stood outside the bar smoking and finishing our road soda. JB looked agitated. The mix of booze, the fight, and all the coke were good gas for the angry fire he had inside him.

"I want to fight," JB said.

"What?" I asked.

"I want to get into a fight." He put out his smoke. "I'm going to go into the bar and start a fight."

"You'll get killed."

"How do you know?"

"Because, I'd get killed if I did that and I could kick your ass."

"Then we should fight," he said.

"Ok," I said. "Let's go home first." I pointed up the street. A police car had arrived. It sat parked, with its lights flashing, on the Phi-Lo side of the intersection.

"I'm going to kick your fat ass." JB walked towards me and knocked his shoulder into mine as he passed. I'd never been in a fight before, scuffles sure, but nothing like what we saw at the Portal. I followed closely behind JB. He turned a few times to mock me. It was like he was an athlete pumping himself up for a big game. I stayed quiet and seethed. I thought about how he threw those panties in my face. I thought about the night after my first date with Martha. I told JB how much I liked her, I told him that I was really going to try and make a go of it with Martha. Then a few weeks later, he was dating her. I thought about other fights I had seen, how angry, and disorganized they were.

Once we got back to the house, JB turned to me. He put his fists up. Normally it would have made me laugh, but I was scared. I mimicked him and put my fists up, too. I scrunched down, pulled into myself as much as I could and moved towards him. JB was a good three inches taller than me and that would give him a better reach. I moved toward him slowly. I started having trouble keeping an eye on him. The street light directly behind him created a blind spot that he disappeared into. His face lost all definition in the silhouette and it was difficult to make out the edges of his body. I squinted, hoping that would help my vision, but it did nothing. I raised my hand to block the light and I guess JB took that for a first punch. He started to swing. One of his punches landed. I took it better than I expected. He'd hit me on my skull, the left side above my temple. It seemed he did more damage to his hand than my head because he shook it after he hit me. I threw my first punch. He was just out of reach, it landed softly on his chest. He let out a laugh. He swung and caught me again, this time in the chest. It took a bit of my air.

When he was in the blind spot I could only guess where his head was. I moved left, nervous that the next punch was going to land square on my nose. I found I could see better, I kept moving clockwise until the light was behind me. Finally, I had good eyes on him. I could see him in sharp focus and knew the light was giving him as much trouble as it gave me. He panicked and started swinging wildly. I took a step back. It was that easy to avoid him. I pulled my right fist back, stepped toward him and put all my weight into the punch. I caught him right in the face, just below his eye. He stutter-stepped backwards and then fell towards me with his hands out. He grabbed onto my shirt as he fell. I was wearing this nine dollar short-sleeve button down I bought from *Target*. For some reason I found myself supremely concerned by the prospect of it being ripped by JB. I decided to just let myself fall with him, in order to save the shirt. I hit the pavement with JB. Instantly something felt wrong. We were face to face on the pavement. He was completely unconscious. I got to my feet. My left arm was pulled close to my body and my forearm was across my chest, as if I was in a sling. There was a sharp pain in my shoulder. I tried to move it, wiggle it around, but the pain grew more severe. I had no say in how my left arm sat on my body. I felt my shoulder with my right hand, a bone protruded out of the socket.

I started to tell myself to be calm and cool. *Be cool, be cool, be cool, breathe,* I repeated. I needed a doctor. I nudged JB with my foot, just shook him a little. He didn't wake. I rolled him onto his back and saw that his face was bloody. My *be cool* mantra changed to *I'm fucked, I'm fucked, I'm fucked, breathe.* I knelt down to examine him and try to see where the blood was coming from. It didn't appear to be gushing out, although his hair was pretty wet with the stuff. He must have hit his head on the pavement in the fall, but I couldn't tell exactly where the cut was. It wasn't from the punch. That was clear. A little red welt had started to blossom under his eye. I started off towards the staircase that led to our front door, but turned back, realizing I couldn't leave JB unconscious in the street. With just one good arm, it was difficult to move his body. I grabbed him by the wrist and pulled, but my new knowledge of how easily shoulders could be dislocated made me think I could just pop his arm out. I grabbed a bunched-up fistful of his shirt, no better. Finally I stuck my hand in his pants and grabbed him by the belt and waist band. My panic was growing. I abandoned any attempt to move him gingerly. In a few exhausting heaves I had him over the curb and on the sidewalk. I ran in the house and grabbed a tee shirt that had been left hanging over the back of the couch, and a bag of frozen Brussels sprouts from the freezer and went back out. JB was sitting up when I returned.

"You ok?" I asked. He seemed pretty out of it and smiled when he saw me.

"Do you think my mom is happy?" he asked. I helped him to his feet and held onto him as he got his balance. He grimaced and tentatively touched his head with his hand, and then examined the blood on his fingers. "What the fuck?"

"Let's make our way to the hospital," I said. We moved slowly down the sidewalk towards Junipero Sierra Boulevard. The Muni had stopped running and I figured that road was our best chance of finding a cab.

"Who won?" JB asked while touching his eye with his bloody hand. His walk steadied and the blank expression on his face had given way to a more focused look of discomfort.

"Draw?" I offered. We took a seat on the bus bench next to the empty boulevard and waited. A few cars sped by after a few empty minutes, no cabs. My shoulder pain became sharper and more pronounced. The beer and the drugs and the adrenalin were wearing off. The shame and regret were kicking in. JB had the bag of Brussels sprouts inside the tee shirt and was holding it to his head. He muttered fuck a couple times and spit.

As I watched him tend to his hurts I knew it was over, all of it. Us as friends, his relationship with Martha, and mine with Zelda. It was just a matter of time. When Martha returned from Chicago, things wouldn't just go back to normal. You don't just have an abortion and then never think of it again. Could she look JB in the face every day without turning over the decision time and time again? Would she be able to go a full day without thinking 'was it JB's baby or was it Ethan's?' And then what? Break it off with JB, shut me out, and Zelda too? Would she try to shove it down and bury it or would she come clean and let everyone know the truth? Martha was a good person, despite all the shitty things she did. She could still mean something to somebody, but not to JB or me or even Zelda. And that meant that I couldn't mean anything to any of them either.

"A while back, Martha asked me if you cheated on her." I said. He leaned forward on the bench and hung his head. "I didn't say you didn't."

"I figured as much," he said. I felt my mouth fill with words, like vomit. I was about to tell him everything. I wanted him to know I was sorry for being so selfish and petty. I stopped my confession before it poured out of me.

"I'm a bad friend," I said.

"You're a fucking asshole." He stood up and raised his free hand. A cab came to a stop in front of the bus stop bench and we got in.

Kelly couldn't fly, she was in her last trimester. I had to go to JB and Martha's wedding alone. I was running late and JB and Martha were already at the altar exchanging vows. Quietly, I took a seat in the last pew. I searched the crowd to see if I spotted any familiar faces. They seemed to be all strangers to me. People started to clap. I looked up and JB and Martha were kissing, married. Everyone stood and I spotted Zelda, a few pews in front of me. She turned with a smile to the man next to her. She touched the small of his back and he leaned over to kiss her on cheek. I was happy to see her happy, after all the shit I put her through. Then that turned to jealousy when I noticed her looking at him with such reverence. I thought of a few things I could say to them at the reception that would cool those stolen glances.

To growing applause JB and Martha walked down the central aisle. They looked happy in that dreamy kind of way that you only see in the photographs that come in picture frames. I lifted my hand to them as they passed by, but neither seemed to register my presence. I stepped into the receiving line and waited anxiously amongst the other attendees. They were standing shoulder to shoulder, just outside of the church. JB shook my hand firmly when I greeted him. Martha smiled. She looked genuinely pleased to see me.

"Congratulations," I said and gave him a one-armed hug. "Thanks for inviting me and Kelly, she's real sorry to miss it."

"Congratulations to you, too," JB said. "I can't believe you are going to be a father. That poor kid."

"I know, right?" I said and looked at Martha. "Congratulations, to you, my dear." I kissed her on the cheek. There was no sign on her face that she was at all uncomfortable with the three of us being together. I wondered if she ever came clean and told him or if it was just something they silently agreed never to speak of. "Well, I'm very happy for you two. And thanks for having me here. It means a lot to me."

"Let's knock a few back at the reception, like the old days," JB said.

"That would be great," I said and as I turned to step away JB wouldn't let go of my hand. He pulled me towards him, hugged me again. I patted him on the shoulder and we smiled at each other and it felt like we'd moved on, once again, but better this time. I walked down the front steps of the church, through the crowd, across the street and got into the back of the cab and headed back to the airport.

Jack Ridl

A Week After

The boys, eight and seven,
have gone home with their father.
Tonight he will read to them

for the first time, opening
to the page where there
is a bookmark with

an elephant drawn on it.
Tomorrow he will learn
which son wants only

Rice Chex and which
wants no jelly but blueberry
on his wheat toast.

Jack Ridl

Instead of Planting Roses

He'd work the garden until dark,
now and then looking up

to see if she was looking out
the window. She'd loved roses.

After two years, he gave up,
started sleeping on the left side,

and instead of planting roses,
filled the plot with tomatoes,

beans, zucchini, and asparagus.
The next year he added eggplant

then mixed in impatiens, pansies,
obedient plant, asters, autumn joy.

He loved to be surprised by a tomato
showing up within a mass of lobelia,

to discover peas climbing a tangle
of cosmos, lilies, and cleome,

to find a squash under the geraniums.

Jack Ridl

She's Selling Their Bed

Yesterday the Forest Farm catalogue lay
in wait in our post office box. Its arrival,
a holiday for those of us tired of shoveling
snow, scraping the car's windows, leaving
our shoes on a mat just inside the door.

Imagine: a catalogue that can bring
a hopeless sense of renewal. Within
234 pages in furrows of lists they've
sown more than 100,000 descriptions
of desire's undying possibilities: reds,

yellows, mauve, green, so much green:
stems, leaves, buds ready to open
into the relentless surprise of flower.
At the local nursery, "The Magic Grower,"
we once asked for a Japanese Maple. "We

have four." This catalogue's madness
describes over 200 varieties: Inazuna,
Hagaromor, Green Mist, Beni Hoshi.
We could roam within a maple forest
from Autumn Fire to Yellow Bird. I want

everything, every "Ornamental And Useful
Plant From Around The World." This
morning, skimming through the classifieds,
I saw that she's selling their bed. After
they first saw our haphazard hope

for a cottage garden, he went right home,
searched online, and ordered more than
100 perennials. The next day he ripped up
the grass and elegantly carved a dozen beds
at the edge of the shade of their unknown maple.

Jack Ridl

Sunday Sermons

Reverend Kirkson gave
five sermons in a row on
abstinence. By the fifth,
alcohol, we were ready
to follow him everywhere,
sure we'd catch him
taking a swig, a puff,
sneaking a long look,
anything. We never did.
So, we'd leaf our way
through *Playboy*, steal
a pack of Camels,
laugh about his kids,
and imagine Christ himself
tapping him on the shoulder,
and when he turned, the Lord
would hand him a cigar, then
tell him to go home and
make his wife. We loved
each horny minute of our dream.
Six months later, he left our
town. We heard he'd screwed
a dozen wives. We laughed
and swore there really was a God.

Jack Ridl

What Are You Supposed to Do Anyway?

Trying to know what to do is difficult
enough, let alone knowing what to do

anyway. I could take that at least two ways,
maybe more. For example, I could take a walk,

even a long walk and I would expect to walk
through the woods or a field or a park or downtown.

But what if I didn't take a walk and instead just kept
the walk to myself, kept it here amidst all the indecision

about where to take that walk? I might pop open a brew,
kick off my hiking boots, put on a smoking jacket

and pile up some Jane Austen and some Henry James,
just pile them up. And then maybe I'd talk with you

even though you are no longer here. It could be like that,
or maybe it is like that. And at night the sky would be full

of the same stars as the night before last. At least it seems
    that way.

Rebecca Chace

Catskill Series

CAKE:

The first summer it was cake. It was his birthday, and as the Girlfriend I wanted to make him a cake. The problem was that he thought a proper cake had to be made from scratch (he is from Iowa, where they apologize if they use a mix). I'm from New York, where we order out Chinese and I don't remember my mother ever baking a cake. She probably did a couple of times, but it would have been over the top to look any farther than those helpful drawings on the back of the box: one egg, a tablespoon of vegetable oil and half a cup of water. I grew up in a household where you opened the refrigerator to find a bottle of ice water in the jar that used to be filled with orange juice. We weren't poor; my mother just wasn't super organized about food. I got my after-school snacks at the corner store, and heated up a can of "Spaghetti-O's" for dinner. At my father's apartment it was frozen food: fish sticks and chicken pot pie. We never had dessert at either of my parent's places, though nobody was trying to lose weight (perhaps unsurprisingly, we were all quite thin). My father used to say "desserts are for other people" as a joke, and it *was* kind of funny, but I couldn't help but wonder why we weren't those other, dessert kind of people.

I compensate as an adult by routinely over-buying whenever I have people over for dinner. I love to cook, but I cook for twenty, when there are ten. My boyfriend's mother baked so frequently that she saved the wax paper covering from the butter sticks to grease the pan for the next batch of cookies. I am trying to remember sticks of butter from my childhood but all I come up with are small plastic tubs of margarine.

I may not bake, but I depend upon toast.

I am also good at dinner, great at salads and that usually works out fine because my boyfriend is famous for his homemade pies. Still, it was his birthday, the first of his birthdays that we ever celebrated together, and nobody wants to bake their own cake. He has a July birthday that usually finds him at his farmhouse in the Catskills. I was treading carefully in this house, not because it is fancy, it's disheveled the way a country house is supposed to be. I was being careful because we were not alone: every move I made was being watched by his adolescent son and his wife. The boy pretended not to notice anything I did, but I knew he never missed a beat—once upon a time I had also been a teenager with my father's girlfriend in the kitchen. The wife watched from a framed photo and snapshots on the refrigerator. She had died a year and a half earlier after a long, hard cancer. She had been ill for nearly half of her son's lifetime, and this was the second July birthday without her. I was the first girlfriend. He let slip that his wife had been excellent at baking cakes, and since I was intimidated by piecrusts, perhaps I could specialize in cakes instead.

I was doomed from the start, and truth be told, I don't even like cake.

I chose what looked like a simple vanilla cake from *The Joy of Cooking*, and there was a bundt pan, which was somewhat intimidating but would make it look more festive. The night before his birthday, I layered the sides of the bundt pan with so much butter we could have greased many cookie pans. (I saved the wrappers for him). Miraculously, the cake rose as promised, and after a few moments of extreme anxiety when I turned over the pan (I was alone in the kitchen, certain that I would have to claw the cake out in pieces and stick it all back together somehow) the whole thing slid onto the cooling rack looking exactly like one of those comforting line drawings. I felt like a genius. But I was only halfway there. There was still the frosting. I had never even heard of frosting from scratch. At least cakes were made from recognizable ingredients like flour, baking soda and eggs. I didn't really know what frosting was made of, but had the uncomfortable feeling that lard might be involved. Frosting is one of those things that taste better the less you know about how they are made, like pork rinds.

There were so many recipes for frosting that I had to consult with the expert. But my boyfriend didn't know much about frosting, the birthday cakes had always been made by his wife. (Right.) He called his sister-in-law, and I felt my incompetence growing as I imagined the series of family calls and emails that would arise from this one conversation. His wife's large family has been welcoming and gracious, and I am quite certain that when they met me they gave no thought to birthday cake, but still ... she can't make frosting? The sister assured us that the "No Fail" white frosting from *The Joy of Cooking* would be a snap.

It is possible to fail at "No Fail" frosting.

I stood over that pot, stirring madly, pouring in more and more confectioner's sugar—actually, no—I am exaggerating for dramatic effect. I followed the recipe exactly ... and failed completely. It was white and hard and broke apart the smooth flanks of the bundt cake as I tried to spread it with a rubber spatula. I managed to press it over most of the cake, then dressed up the blank spots with fresh flowers. My boyfriend assured me that it was beautiful.

It was not beautiful.

I have a photograph of him blowing out the candles with his son watching and their expressions are not ones that I would associate with a Happy Birthday. The cake tasted fine (if you like cake) and over the next few days there were white chips in the refrigerator that fell off the sides of the cake like peeling paint. The boy saw to those. I couldn't bear to look at it.

That was the first summer.

CHAIRS:
I have been painting chairs this summer. It is my second summer at his house in the Catskills, though it's not only my boyfriend's house. The house belongs to him and his wife, and her death still feels as blunt and brutal as the undeniable fact that the phrase "passed away" is trying to soften.

The house is filled with photos of her, the two of them with their son, aglow with the happiness of a good marriage. They had one child and the sense I get is that this boy completed their world. The three of them created a perfect geometry for each other. I also have adolescent children, but their father is alive. He and I were not the perfect geometry for each other and there are no framed photos of my married life in my home anymore.

The bedroom has a special place for her, a shrine he has made in this era of non-denominational invention. There are photos of her, photos of the two of them, and objects of personal significance: a postcard, a shell. I don't need to ask or be told the stories there. I know enough of grieving to understand there is no linear time here. Since the shrine is under the window opposite the bed it is the first thing I see every morning when I wake up. I wondered if the shrine would still be in the bedroom this summer when I came to spend a month in the country. When I saw that it was, I said nothing. I am sleeping with her as well.

I would be even if the shrine was packed away.

We both have dreams about her. Guilty dreams—he will dream that she is still alive but he is having an affair with me. I dream that I just found out he is married, and I can't believe I've been so stupid (again). Sometimes my dreams are driven by jealousy. She is calling on the phone and the two of them are laughing at jokes that come of a shared history, he is running to get his son to speak to her. In this dream I am in the room but he is not thinking about me at all; he simply ignores me.

I am painting chairs. I found some old chairs in the barn and had the idea that putting them around this rough property would be an invitation to sit and look at the stream, or read by the pond. It would be a surprise to visitors, an unexpected color. My boyfriend is an abstract painter but this is my project. He watched me forget to prime a dark wooden chair and said nothing as I layered on three coats of yellow paint and still didn't get the smooth enamel I wanted. I buy "mis-mixed" paint for cheap from the hardware store and he makes no comment on my color choices. The chairs get painted and they go outdoors. We joke that it's my art installation, and when a new one is finished I surprise him with where I've placed it in the landscape. He says it makes him happy to see the chairs. He says that I make him happy.

Of course we talk about her. I talk about my ex and we talk about our children. This is real life and we no longer have the fearlessness of youth, when you moved in together because you were spending every night in each other's arms and the rent was cheaper that way. Sometimes I wish we were both that fearless again, but even if all the children were grown and gone, when he says "we" he usually means himself and his wife.

There are birds that lay eggs in abandoned nests, hermit crabs that grow into the empty shell of another creature. I look down into that circle of twigs and hair, scraps of cloth scavenged from the yard. I wonder if there is room for me here and I try to choose my words carefully, though I sometimes fail and he does as well. We work alone and share the tasks that shape the days: gardening, cooking and washing up. I try to think about the silences between us as negative space in a painting, shaping what is there.

I paint another chair and put it out in the field. He will go on a walk to find it on his own.

CURTAINS:
They were only ten dollars at the yard sale. Five sets of clean lace curtains. I don't know how to work a sewing machine (bobbins break at my approach) but I can sew buttons and patches. I can hem. This summer we were playing house. He had the kitchen painted for the first time since he and his wife bought the place, over twenty years earlier. After the paint job, he didn't put every photo and postcard back exactly where they had been before she died. He finally bought a new stove after living with only two burners for who knows how long. It was a country house after all, and he had been paying attention to more important things. Like learning how to grieve. How to have a second life. I am not a widow, but I have my own portion of grief. We are not married.

We are good for each other, but being together is a full-on grown-up pursuit.

We both get tired sometimes.

Curtains seemed like something I could do.

I spread them across the table on the newly painted back porch and tried very hard to measure them correctly, since cutting anything in a straight line is not my area of expertise. I asked about a sewing kit, and he found a round tin that was filled with tiny spools of wool from Saks Fifth Avenue. His wife's family came from money, and many of their things were from her parents' "Big House" that had been sold years earlier. I looked at these miniature skeins of wool and figured they must have bought all of their socks and sweaters from Saks, and this was the extra thread given to match in case the maid needed to darn a hole. There were entwined blends from crimson to heather blue, and stamped onto each cardboard spool were the words "Made in England." Lovely and utterly useless when it came to hemming curtains.

I had remembered to get a spool of white thread at the hardware store, but hadn't bought any needles or pins. Digging around in the bottom of the tin, I found six straight pins. All rusty but serviceable. Then I remembered something left in the top drawer of her bureau that he cleared out for me, a travel sewing kit, the complimentary kind that comes with a hotel room. I had noticed it when I opened the drawer to put away my clothes, but like so many things in this house, I left it untouched.

I brought it downstairs and inside was one needle, along with a colorful array of thread, just enough to sew the one white button that is thoughtfully included in these kits. There were also two brand new straight pins: a treasure trove. I showed my boyfriend, wanting to be sure it was all right to use (I try to be careful not to make assumptions. When our father died my sister didn't want to change the shower curtain long after he would have replaced it himself). My boyfriend said it was fine and that he remembered that little sewing kit. I decided not to ask.

I had to cut and pin one curtain at a time since I had only eight straight pins. I had to be very careful not to lose the one needle. Of course we could have gone to the store, but we try to avoid forays into the neighboring towns. The house is in a part of the Catskills that his friends have dubbed "three hours from anywhere" and that is part of the appeal. There is no internet and no cell phone service and we like it that way. Much better for writing and painting. We eat out of the garden and discourage houseguests. I didn't want to lose half a day driving to town, and in fact I could hem a curtain perfectly well with one needle and eight straight pins. Though the one needle did become a bit of a joke: panic ensued when I thought I lost it, and great celebration when I randomly looked down at the wooden crate that serves as a bedside table and saw a long sewing needle between the cracks. It was old and blackened but much easier to thread than the needle I had been using. He gave me steel wool to clean off the rust, and I wallowed in the luxury of two sewing needles.

Playing house is a tricky business. One of the things I didn't talk about was a previous boyfriend who also cleared a garden for me and provided a writing room. I didn't talk about my married life; a yard with my own garden of lettuce, kale and nasturtiums. All of these lives came to an abrupt end. I am not always good at knowing when to pull off the road at the next exit. Whenever I leave this house at the end of my stay I am careful to leave no trace of my presence behind. I could make curtains, but as I sewed I also thought, I can leave these here if it comes to that. An offering to a house that has given me the complicated gift of time.

We put up the curtains on my final weekend and he admired them as I wondered what his wife would have thought. I packed my things to go back to the city and was putting the travel kit back in the drawer when I stopped: tucked neatly beneath each thread was a brand new, unused sewing needle. There were five colors in the kit and each came with its own sewing needle, threaded and ready to go. How had I missed that abundance? I stuck the blackened needle into the spool of white thread and left it behind as well; a nomad in the land of plenty.

COLORED CHALK:

Tap, tap. Scrape, scrape. The sound of footsteps back and forth, water being poured and every now and then the sound of paint being dripped or sprayed onto canvas. Tap, tap. Scrape, scrape. There was a deeply resonant voice narrating an audio book; later in the afternoon there would be a mix tape or maybe one of those incisive interviews with a bestselling author or movie star on NPR. He had closed the door to his studio and I had my earplugs in but there was no real soundproofing possible. This was an actual barn, not a refurbished one with skylights and insulated walls. When he and his wife bought the place he cut holes in the walls and put in windows from an abandoned loft building downtown— they put up some sheetrock and clip lights and they were good to go. That was their honeymoon. Since she was also a painter, she probably listened to music and books right along with him. Painting together, tending their garden and raising their only child; it was one long soundtrack of inspiration.

Until the cancer, until at some point it was no longer any fun at all.

I stared again at my computer screen. I got up and stretched, not wanting to allow myself to leave my studio. I loved the barn with its many entrances and exits. I even liked the woodpecker jackhammering every morning on the red walls up near the peak of the roof, and this summer there was a woodchuck family dug under one wall, their entrance hidden by a clump of blue asters. My boyfriend left the door to his studio open all night, paintings leaning against the walls or lying on the floor. I asked him what happens if an animal comes in and walks on the canvas? He didn't think that would be a problem for the work. Birds sometimes swooped right through my studio. I propped the doors open to let in the light because it was often cold—the cement-floored milk shed was also the coolest spot in the barn. His studio looked over a field of alfalfa and got light all day, and anyway he never felt the cold.

I would rather swim in the pond, I would rather weed the garden, in fact, I would rather clean the bathroom floor at this point. It wasn't that he was making too much noise for me to work, I was simply jealous. I wanted to paint. I wanted to stride around in paint splattered shorts and flip flops, looking all loose limbed and sexy and never getting cold. I wanted to spend my work day listening to music and audio books rather than being the person who wore sweaters in summertime and couldn't write when there was music with lyrics. It was a nonstop party in his studio; it was a frigid, barren wasteland in mine. It wasn't fair that I had zero artistic ability and hardly knew how to speak about painting. I look at art a lot. I like some things better than others. But I have learned that artists don't like it if you say that a shape reminds you of some object that exists in the world, a cloud for example, or a tree. I not only can't make art, it's really best if I don't talk too much about it. Encouraging murmurs are appreciated. On the other hand, pretty much everyone can read, and a four year old can tell you if your story has a beginning, middle and end.

Encouraging murmurs are appreciated.

The walls of the milk shed are whitewashed cement. Outside, there was a stub of red chalk on the windowsill that had been there all summer, half melted by the rain. I picked it up and drew on the lintel of the door, just a small red mark. Then I made it a little bigger, figuring I could always rub it out. I started to color on the windowsill itself, figuring nobody would really notice and it would disappear in the next big rainstorm. I walked back into my studio and looked at the white wall opposite my writing table. Even though he called it my studio, I had only alighted recently in this place. Unlike painters writers don't need much. A table, a chair, a lamp. I can even do without electricity. I would leave no trace when I left this room. Sometimes I thought that I would feel like a guest here for the rest of my life and I wasn't sure how I felt about that. It was something I was trying not to make any decisions about right now.

Right now, I wanted a whole bucket of colored chalk.

He took an old door and painted it with blackboard paint because it would give me a smoother surface than the cement wall. He hung it up for me and found some fat sticks of chalk from his son's childhood art supplies. He gave me a rag to wipe things away when I wanted to change it. I drew my book.

H. L. Hix

Sex Is Turquoise

It's not so hard to understand. Small town,
        post-war Germany,
beautiful young woman stands looking in a bookstore window,

        debonair, slightly older Turkish man,
           beautiful himself,
speaks to her. *Fräulein* ... She corrects him: *Frau*. Nod of apology.

        She's walking, to escape even briefly
           the few narrow rooms
above her husband's father's bakery, where she lives with her

        quiet husband and his loud family.
           She's known her husband
since they were children, known always she would be married to him,

        passed up a scholarship to music school
           to stay at his side,
but not forgotten dreams of travel she knows she can't fulfill.

        So when they meet again at the market
           and he offers—*Frau*
this time—to carry her bags, she accepts with a flustered blush,

        some part of her no less real than the rest
           given life again.
He's careful not to touch her, but would she do him the honor

to meet him next afternoon for coffee,
          a conversation
on her way to or from some errand? He knows a shop nearby.

Once for coffee turns into more than once,
          turns into long walks,
confidences. Her husband works odd hours, and the family—

never time alone. This man meets her eyes,
          he *listens* to her.
After one walk, a chaste goodbye, his cheek barely touching hers.

Another day, coffee and a long talk,
          he takes her fingers
lightly to help her from the chair, and she does not take them back.

Minna Proctor

A Mystic at Heart

"If your mother had brought you for a reading the day you were born," said The Astrologer, "I would have said: Mrs. Proctor, tell this kid that when she gets to '07, she's going to enter into a very nutty time. And nothing in her life is going to go according to schedule, and it's not of her own doing. If before '07, if she settles down in the suburbs and has 2.5 kids and an SUV and 1.2 dogs and a white picket fence and all that stuff, she's just going to end up walking out on her family, saying 'I've had it.'"

So, this was *destined* to be a period of destruction, dismantling, and derangement in my life. There were too many Gods vying for predominance. I couldn't be true to any of them; I couldn't be partial to some of them. They all had contradicting imperatives: take heed of your mortality, live large, lighten up, get serious, fall in love, date a lot, get married, have kids, travel, laugh, cry, feel shame, stop living for other people, buy shoes, be thrifty, go barefoot, cut the cord, hang tight. Or, as The Astrologer put it, "You're in a crucible of chaos."

My Brooklyn neighborhood was kind of like a suburb. I didn't have the white picket fence and 2.5 kids, but I did have a new marriage to a man I'd been with for a long time and loved entirely, I'd recently published a book, I was in excellent health, I was on boards of charitable organizations and a Jewish group, the house was tidy and attractive, our cat was a stunner, my family was proud of me, I was proud of me. And then I did just pick up and leave. And I had a baby—and my mother died. Everything that I didn't know about life converged on this astonishing moment. It's Pluto's fault. He kills everything so that it can be reborn.

I am a skeptic. The Astrologer confirmed it: "In youth, your chart is that of the disbeliever," he said, "the one who doesn't want to give over, the one who asks a lot of questions, too many questions."

Or I was a skeptic. "The older you get," he continued, "the more this turns into the chart of the mystic."

I was a communist at four; a sharp-tongued atheist by fifteen; at twenty-five, I was, like my mother, occasionally curious about but essentially uninterested in Judaism except with regard to the Holocaust. I was also at this time transitioning out of a collegiate aversion to identity politics and into an incipient sentimental yearning for "family" (though I didn't know yet exactly what I meant by that). When I turned thirty, my father, whom I worshipped but lived too far away from, told me he wanted to become an Episcopal priest. The depth of his spiritual life and religious convictions came as an embarrassing surprise to me—a demonstration of how partially I was involved in his vast second life, and my first intimate encounter with the unique and often urgently private nature of religious experience. Shamefully, I understood nothing about his spirit or religion, or how it fit into our tenuously shared adult life. I wrote a book about it—about faith, the language of faith, what it meant to him, what it did and didn't mean to me as I understood it, what I inherited of his lapsed and regained Christianity, how very much I shared of my mother's secular and sporadically spiritual Judaism. For me, the whole subject was essentially unexplored intellectual territory: philosophy with consequence and conviction, philosophy with ambition.

My book editor kept describing the project as a quest. I kept resisting that descriptive; it seemed too syndicated-UHF-television for me. I wasn't struggling with a quest as much as I was reveling in a burgeoning impression of what having answers might feel like. The religious discussions I was having while researching my book began to provide a kind of clearinghouse for all of my basic adult concerns: Why did I believe in marriage even after my parents had made such mash of theirs? Why did I prize family even though mine was only partially functional? What purpose the life of the mind? Where did I fit into what? And so on.

The Judaism of my demographic—the Judaism I found while working on my book—was wildly appealing. It seduced the sentimental skeptic in me: community-driven, well-oiled, white collar, and doggedly intellectual. Praying stood in for studying, hard questions had answers in textual riddles, and the moral structure seemed earthy and practical. It was a world of listservs and boisterous children, and well-appointed homes stuffed with books, wine, and (sometimes) salami. It was hard not to love it, hard not to feel secure in that world, to feel as if you were going to be OK, no matter how anarchic your past, how insecure your professional world, how deeply ingrained your patterns of confusion, how manipulative your mother, or how mortal.

This was, in no small sense, a palpable model of everything I hoped for from my life. I never wanted a big bling ring or a white princess dress, I just desperately wanted an intact family. The Jews had a strategy: honor the mind, cherish your family, do good in the world. It was almost like a science of hope.

And then everything collapsed. After a fifteen-year battle, my mother's breast cancer metastasized to her skin and collarbone. My fiancé slept with someone else, and so we got married. He took a job in another state I didn't want to go to. I had an affair with a married man, and he left his wife and I left my husband. I got pregnant, had a baby. My mother died. The bricks and mortar of my dream fell away. I cried for a year. I felt like I was losing my mind. As far as doing good—I might as well have lashed a bayonet to my forehead. All that high-minded Jewishness puckered and curled back from the surface, a shiny, heat-resistant veneer.

"So," The Astrologer said, "the first God competing for your attention is Saturn. Saturn is all about mortality. He's the responsible one, the mature one. He's the stern voice of your conscience; he's about shame and guilt. He's saying, 'Get your act together ... Get married, have children.'"

My husband and I had been engaged for a year and were regularly attending a Judaism 101 for Adults class when we approached the rabbi about getting married with a Jewish ceremony. I was an eager but unlearned Jew; he was an open-minded atheist. The rabbi didn't always perform mixed marriages but made an exception for us. We promised to raise our eventual children Jewish (as opposed to nothing).

We agreed on a lot of things (meatballs, Hugo Boss, Naples), but I think our mutual desire for stability came to rest on this hyperfunctional brand of Judaism. It was Norman Rockwell compared to how we'd been brought up, charming and optimistic. It gave us confidence in our future.

When my husband told me he'd had sex with someone else—a revelation that came on the heels of the news about my mother's failing health—he said to me, "I've ruined our life." I rushed to reassure him. I believed that the life we'd built was too strong to be ruined. I guess I'd also believed that he would never do that to me.

There was the most peculiar moment, soon after that, when we went to the rabbi's house to talk about the wedding. Sitting with the rabbi in his living room, chatting about family, instructional books to read, useful Judaica to acquire, and dates—my husband said that he thought he might want to convert. Despite all the studying and signing on to a Jewish wedding and children, I hadn't ever considered the possibility of a full conversion. I responded with amazement, "But you're an atheist!"

What I really wanted to say was, "But you cheated on me!"

"Yeah," he agreed, "but I've been thinking I might be interested."

I think what he wanted to say was that he wanted to heal us. It was a gesture; *he* believed in us. That big-hearted, hapless, cynical misanthrope found faith in *us*.

Our secret seemed so potent there, then. As if it had a life of its own, and if I didn't clasp my hands very carefully in my lap and keep my legs crossed just so, it might spill out everywhere.

What neither of us said was that we wanted to regain control of a situation that had started spinning out of control. We agreed on so much. We agreed to pretend it had never happened.

"This period might have begun with you having a great deal of security—thinking that you knew what was going on, what was about to happen," The Astrologer said. "Then lo and behold, your whole world got shaken, making one of your greatest fears come true. 'Oh my God, I was blind. Oh my God, I got hoodwinked. Oh my God, I pulled the wool over my eyes' ... Which is one of your worst fears, if not the worst fear. It's very humiliating for you."

Pedophiles, I firmly believe, do not enter the priesthood with the goal of gaining access to young boys. Quite the opposite. Yes, they're drawn to the purity, as well as the reassurance of the familiar, the regular structure of the day. But they also come to this life because they want to get better. They want to be better, purer than they are, holier than they are. Fortresses. It is so striking that the most incurable criminal disorder afflicts a disproportionate number of men of the cloth. Something beyond the allure of altar boys brought these men to their place. It is the promise of sanctity, the protection of sanctity. To live with the angels is to assume their ways—no? Just as laughing when you're sad can make you feel better.

I wonder now whether I was attracted to that particular cosmopolitan expression of Judaism precisely because it was what I aspired to yet was most incapable of.

My husband told me that I set standards for myself that I didn't live up to. I wanted to be good, moral, generous, diligent, loving, sensitive, loyal, dependable, reassuring, ambitious, successful, healthy, innovative, vibrant. I wanted to make a family, be a good daughter, a good friend, a good writer, a good provider. I wanted to find peace and stability in family life because my own family had been emotional mayhem. I wanted to be happily married. My standards were high; I wanted to walk with the angels.

But I had an affair. I ended my marriage. Dashed my own hopes (pulled the wool over my own eyes). I'm not an angel, and it wasn't a strategy—or a religion for that matter—that failed me. It was something in me, a disconnect between me and my dreams, some misunderstanding about what was right, about how to be good, a basic misunderstanding. But once upon a time, before I admitted the flaws into my life, I thought religion might save me from them.

"Every revolutionary," wrote the theologian Henri Nouwen, "is challenged to be a mystic at heart and he who walks the mystical way is called to unmask the illusory quality of human society."

I read a lot of Nouwen while I was researching my book. He was the go-to guy for pastoral theology in the 1970s. His concerns are so dated now: he worried about Nuclear Man, the "threat of New Technologies," and hippies. But he was a great pastor and writer because of the resonant clarity with which he explained that ministering to people in need was ultimately about understanding what comfort was and where strength lies. I keep coming back to the idea that there's something fundamentally revolutionary in compassion.

I called Temple Beth Elohim in Wellesley to ask if my mother and I could come to their High Holiday services. Apologizing for the last-minute call, I explained to the woman who answered the phone at the synagogue that my mother was very ill, critically ill, and that I had traveled from out of town to take care of her.

"Are you members?" she asked.

We were members, I told her, twenty-three years ago; my sister and I had our Bat Mitzvahs there. I didn't elaborate on how disappointing it had all been for us. How forbiddingly clubby my mother had found the wealthy community, particularly unwelcoming to a recent divorcée and not especially well-equipped to serve single parents. I made a flimsy, obtuse reference to how we were grown up now and didn't live nearby.

"But you're not currently members," she clarified and then told me that the services were open only to members.

Granted, most synagogues have this policy for the High Holidays. I asked if we could buy tickets.

No.

"Could an exception be made? It's quite urgent," I asked miserably, frustrated with my inability to be direct. I wanted to say that it would be my mother's last Yom Kippur. Instead, I added, "It's very important to us."

She suggested that I try Hillel at one of the nearby colleges. "They often have community services." I had never in my life heard community pronounced as if the word itself were filthy. I didn't know how to explain that we weren't looking for an adventure, that my mother's deteriorating body couldn't possibly bear a folding chair in a drafty function room, or a twenty-minute drive. I didn't argue that nine months pregnant and on twenty-four-hour call to my sick mother, I didn't have the energy to take us somewhere that would require the use of a map, that we were both scared, already ravaged, and needed to be at least somewhere familiar if not friendly. That I couldn't possibly spend the afternoon on the phone tracking down Kol Nidre.

"Do you have children?" she suddenly blurted out. The loophole. The open-house policy of all thriving synagogues: young families shopping around for Hebrew school.

"I'm pregnant," I offered. "So there's children on the way."

"But you don't have any now."

"Not technically."

"Yup," she concluded, "I can't help you."

Suddenly, unexpectedly overcome with anger, I hissed at her, "Well, I'll just have to find us a real Jewish community then, won't I?" I hung up as loudly as I could.

When I asked my father what was so great about the Episcopal Church his answer was that he felt welcome there when he needed it most: isolated, confused, often drunk, and shattered by guilt after the divorce. His church was "a big umbrella." In no small sense the fellow members of his church rescued him by sitting next to him, adding his name to the telephone trees, and arguing local politics with him at picnic potlucks.

Over the past few years, I've heard so many people say some version of: "I believe in God, but I don't believe in *organized* religion." It makes sense; we are a country of individualists, people who don't relish the idea of being herded. Independence aside, though, I'm not sure I understand the point of a one-man religious experience. We are ultimately utterly alone. It's as much a curse as a gift. But we're not prophets, and we don't have to take to the desert. We build communities to take shelter in them: churches, reading groups, support groups, labor unions, mothers for world peace. I don't think I fully comprehended the significance of my father's answer until I found myself out in the darkness, casting about for refuge.

My community on Yom Kippur was my mother and me, alone in that chilly shell of a home—her choking down half a teacup of broth and a spoonful of Percocet in yogurt and me standing over the kitchen sink wolfing down a rubbery slab of leftover mozzarella marinara. In our conditions, neither of us was required to fast, and yet neither of us had the stomach for food. Atonement is just hunger. Remembering the dead—there was nothing to *remember*; we were in it, sitting together in her dimmed bedroom, the dead all around us, our shadows, their echoes, my dying mother, my unborn son, this twilight space between life and death.

"Pluto," continued The Astrologer, "is very intense. Pluto wants to end your life as you have known it, and he doesn't care about whatever your expectations and desires were for yourself. Your life just doesn't mean that much to him. He's going to come along and blow away your dreams. Pluto isn't very nice to humans … and all of this might be very discombobulating. This is all an experiment now, a passage, an improvisation. You have to go with it, see where it takes you. You don't really have a choice. Because, if you're trying to follow the old road, the one you were on, well, it's gone. There's no more road."

Late one night in Italy, as we were trying to navigate a snowy mountain pass and slipping and sliding and whooping with delight each time the heavy old unheated sedan made it over another crest, my husband—long before he was my husband—said to me: "You know, if we ever get divorced, we'll just have to get back together again. That's just the way it is."

God, did that make me feel loved as I never had been.

I repeated the story to my mother one day while we were talking about family, and true to her solipsistic character, she replied, "Your father never said anything like that to me."

He didn't really love her, she said. He was too young, and she knew it. She knew that their age difference would be a problem. She didn't think he knew what love was. She didn't think he really loved her.

But he talked her into it, and she said she was convinced, "because he was a religious man ... once." She didn't know what it was like to be religious like him, and she was seduced by the exoticism of it, the promises hidden beneath the layers of this mysterious creed. He grew up Catholic, he'd been to seminary, he went to church on Sundays. He believed in something bigger, he believed in family, and he understood the meaning of vows. He broke them. He strayed. He had a long dark night of the soul, which in Christianity is often considered a rite of passage. So, was it religion or my father who'd misled her?

She had seen (as I had, as my husband once had) religion as a cloak of protection. What did any of us know? She was a musician, we were writers; we invented stuff. We attributed tremendous creative and sustaining power to the expression of faith. We were vulnerable to religion's promises because we weren't really stuck with it—its failings, inconsistencies, equivocations. When it came to planning a marriage, I think we all put a great deal of stock in the religious system. So we held a Jewish wedding and signed a *ketubbah*, a beautiful hand-lettered contract.

One day when I was feeling brave, I decided to do some research about Jewish divorce—an ancient provision, put into place mostly to protect people from being stuck with a barren partner. I read that we'd have to sign a *get*, another contract, in order to be officially divorced under Jewish law. One of the special caveats of a Jewish divorce is that you are expressly forbidden from remarrying.

Despite everything that's happened since, and how very far we both are from that snowy mountainside, I thought to myself when I read that, "Thank God I don't believe in that bullshit anymore." I know there's no more of the old road, but it was there once, and I was on it, and it is a part of me. I don't have any interest in letting the Jews and their laws or Pluto with his destructive hacksaw strip me of my dreams, even the old ones.

"It's a good time to trust your faith," said The Astrologer, "because there's nothing much in the real world you can rely on. If faith doesn't work, go see art, look at things that are bigger than yourself and your universe."

I wasn't brought up religious, and neither was my mother—or her parents before her. That side of my family is historically made up of socialists, freethinkers, and artists. There's significantly more Jewish pride in my blood than prayer. My mother lost her mother when she was thirteen and turned to music for solace—that's the religion she brought my sister and me up in. We flirted with ritual over the years (especially in dark times), but our collective impressions of it kept falling somewhere between hopeful and suspicious. Our household was an artistic one; I've spent far more Sundays in museums than Friday nights in temple, including this last, recent incursion into Judaism. Shostakovich's Piano Trio No. 2 is irreducible in a way that Genesis isn't—or so it seems to me.

My mother spent fifteen years not dying, and on that point she was unwavering to the end. In order to take care of her during the last few months of her life, my sister and I had to expend enormous energy agreeing with her that she wasn't dying. We shrank our worlds in order to be with her in the way she wanted. We stood in for the home health aides she kept firing because she wasn't dying, we nursed her, tended to the minutiae of her terrible exigencies, deflected the visitors and callers whose valedictory wishes smacked of resignation and betrayal.

"She's been going on fumes for three weeks already," the hospice nurse told us.

"She's in denial," said the social worker. "You have to help her accept this."

"I can only think in black and white," she said one afternoon. And then later that same night, grabbed her best friend's wrist fiercely and said, "Shhh. Don't tell anyone. I'm going to get better."

About a year and a half earlier, my mother had approached my rabbi while on a visit to New York, shyly asking if he would talk to her about a Jewish burial. It was the closest she'd ever come to planning, even admitting, mortality—aside from the promise we had made to her long ago that we would bury her with her down comforter so that she would be warm. It was also an awkward overture to Judaism that she felt comfortable making with me by her side—emboldened, I presume, by *my* inflated sense of security. For some reason the meeting ended up being too difficult to schedule, and the conversation never took place. Before the year was out, she'd become too sick to travel anymore.

Although she never did learn very much about it, my mother was definitive that she wanted a Jewish burial. She wrote that much into her will, but didn't elaborate, tiring easily of the subject. When the hospice rabbi came around for a visit, she summoned the energy to ask again what Jewish burial entailed, but then instantly lost interest. When the rabbi said, "What would you like to know?" my mother just shrugged. I think she wanted the hospice rabbi to tell her that it would be easier to die a Jew. But she was as Jewish as she ever would be, and she already knew without asking that nothing was big enough to make it easier.

I believe she wanted to be taken care of, honored, buried quickly, cleaned, blessed, wrapped in white, deep in sacred ground, an ancient prayer, one repeated across the world: *Yit gadal, v'yit kaddash* ... The Jewish communion of the dead—that strange, massive, and ageless pantheon of *our* dead.

A Jewish burial has to happen quickly: properly, within a day or two. My mother slipped into a coma on Thanksgiving and died late the next night. The funeral home assured us that we had some leeway with the ritual, as it was the Sabbath and we were so totally unprepared. As long as she was being tended to, prayed over, and in the freezer.

Getting into a Jewish cemetery as an unaffiliated Jew turned out to be as difficult as getting into the High Holidays at a tony suburban synagogue. My sister's inquiries at her local Reform cemetery—an elegant parcel of protected, park-like land in Western Massachusetts—proved quickly futile when we realized that it would take days on end to convene the temple board to petition them for an exception to the members-only rule.

The hospice rabbi had suggested the Baker Street Cemetery, vividly describing how the cemetery's sections were divided into synagogues, and unions, and Old World towns—there was even a Workmen's Circle section (my great-grandmother had dedicated her life to the Workmen's Circle). The map of the grounds was like an Isaac Babel story. To be buried there in Yiddish with those distant comrades would be like coming home for my mother.

And so, the day after Thanksgiving, my sister and I bundled my baby and ourselves up as warmly as we could and set out for West Roxbury. Our high hopes were quickly dashed. The cemetery wasn't far enough off Route 128—a row of trees separated it from an auto dealership and a grotty shopping strip beyond that. It was a forbiddingly tidy and arid place, especially on that very gray, subzero afternoon. When I dutifully called the director of the graveyard to find out if there was even a possibility of putting our mother there, he gamely replied that we'd probably have to join the Workmen's Circle and make a plea for special dispensation to be placed in that section. I barely listened to his by now somewhat predictable response. We already knew that we hated it there, and it had nothing to do with anything beyond the fact that my mother would have hated it, too. It was ugly.

The cemetery where we ended up, a beautiful historical forested hill right out of Amherst Center, was perfect—not at all what we thought we were looking for, and not Jewish, though there are Jews buried there—the renegades and atheists. Wildwood Cemetery hosts an eclectic crowd of locals, professors, and artists. A large statue of a bucking horse marks the grave right next to our mother's resting place up on a wooded hill, the perfect vantage point from which to watch a winter sunset. Behind my mother's plot, there is a swath of elaborate benches marking graves from the last hundred years, each lovingly and haphazardly arranged among the trees. Quirky affairs, like my mother: one bright white marble bench, guarded by leonine gargoyles and looking like something Salvador Dali might have painted into the scenery, bears the admonition *Watch It*.

Meanwhile, I was on the phone with the funeral directors, trying to negotiate the hiring of a rabbi for the funeral. No slight matter, as it seems that especially on a Saturday morning over the Thanksgiving weekend, any rabbi worth his salt is either unreachable or unavailable. The funeral director finally ended our search for the perfect rabbi on short notice with the suggestion, "Look, I've got someone who can surely do the service for you; he's a local cantor who's always up for anything."

I wanted a rabbi worthy of my mother—someone who wouldn't patronize her, or us, by pretending to know us. Someone who could honor her with the simple ancient ritual that she had wanted. I wanted someone unique and brilliant, not freelance. I was ever so mercifully wrong.

Cantor Morton Shames called the next afternoon to talk about the service. When I told him that my mother was a complicated woman and that it was very important to us that he not pretend he knew her, he gently replied that he understood. For well over an hour, I tried to explain my mother to him, as if it were the most important portrait I would ever paint, miserably trying to sift the most salient details from seventy-two years of life. My sister and I, independently rambling on over the phone to this unfamiliar craggy voice, both ended up describing my mother as an aesthete—

so thoroughly consumed with the pursuit of beauty that often her feet didn't touch the ground. This held true as much for the music she wrote as for the way she arranged flowerpots in the corner of a room, as for the intent way she listened to a friend. Cantor Shames interjected with quiet exclamations—"How wonderful!" "I wish I could have met her."

The funeral was not Jewish in the strictest sense, but of course, neither was my mother. It was, however, the funeral she was meant to have.

As he stood by her plot on that cold, wet morning, flipping through a thick stack of index cards upon which he'd meticulously composed his sermon in pencil, it became utterly clear that no one but Cantor Shames could have honored our mother better. He understood her, through us, and what she meant to us, and that mattered. More than that, he seemed to have received, through means I'll never understand, a profound appreciation of her music. His voice, a bold, weeping tenor, cracking under the weight of the mourner's prayers, lifted to the sky. He blew the music up there and then carried her, too, up past the treetops, and he took her away. She was really gone.

I am a Jewish mother now, as my mother was before me, and her mother before her—Jewish, not quite Jewish. Another generation in the family that never really has found company in the house of the Lord. We're park dwellers: instinctual, undisciplined, two degrees isolated from the world we live in.

My mother was clingy, indulgent, petulant, and maudlin. Her love was demanding, sometimes contractual, almost unbearably consuming. Throughout the fifteen years she spent fighting cancer, it was consistently impossible to get a straight report from her about her health; we'd have to rely on the most eccentric coterie of intermediaries for news. The good patches were fairy tales; the scary patches were a secret. When she'd get sick, my sister and I would come running to her side. Every time, whatever she needed. We were a small family. The three of us made it up as we went along. My mother taught me everything: to fight, to survive, to love for dear life. And everything that she taught me, my son has let me feel.

Isaac was named for laughter—that's his burden. When God told Sarah that she was to be a mother at 101 years old, she fell to the ground laughing, hilarious with disbelief. I wasn't supposed to be a mother this way either: too late, in the midst of a betrayal, a collapse, a long, painful death, the disintegration of my plans, ideas, dreams, this crucible of destruction. I wasn't supposed to be a mother like this. But Isaac was meant to be.

The moment of revelation is absurdly clear in my memory: I was sitting on the edge of the tub, washing clothes in a bucket. I adjusted the hot water and let it run over my hands, thinking that the only thing I knew was that I had to have my baby. I can't have been more than three months pregnant, and I was so profoundly confused about every single thing going on in my life that the sudden feeling of conviction was startling. My son was never a choice. Stopping the pregnancy was never an option, and how I felt about the baby was already more than how I'd ever felt about anything. It was love or truth, an absolute belief in the invisible. It was religion. Now I understand.

I underestimated faith. I looked for it in the wrong places, such mundane places—I looked for it in books, in rituals, in gatherings of people. But that's religion for people who have it. I hit the limits of that kind of faith the moment I strayed from the plan. It was all there; then it was dust.

The Astrologer says I'm not out of the woods; there won't be any order in my particular configuration of stars for some time to come. Pluto, Saturn, Uranus, and Neptune are all still lording over me, fighting for dominance. In my own gimpy, flailing way, I've been answering to all of them, and none. My son was born three weeks before my mother died. Time enough for her to see him alive; time for her to realize that seeing him wasn't enough; time enough for her to forget him and forget the sadness of losing him to the future; and time for me to watch my mother and my son exchange places. For three weeks, these two helpless, overwhelmed creatures had the same desperate faraway look in their eyes. They spent three weeks watching each other—time enough for eternity.

Per Šmidl

We Belonged Together

Per Šmidl lived in a wagon in Copenhagen's Christiania for two years. His autobiographical novel describes living there among people with an individual and original approach to life, curious tourists, anarchists and whatever category you can think of.

This is how we talked about these things. There was nothing to be done about it. For as long as we were married, Christiania remained a touchy issue. The Freetown opened a split in my wife's personality that was a source of pain. Yet, as I have tried to point out, the pain was not pure. Things were complicated by the joy mixed in with it. She readily admitted it was fun when we visited our friends in The Gunpowder House provided it only happened once in a while (*and* there was a safe haven we could return to). Not that she ever mentioned it when we were in Christiania, but at home, it never failed that she complained about the junk scattered everywhere in the Freetown. It was because of the "visible chaos," she said, that she would not ever dream of living there. It was dangerous too. You could easily get into trouble, especially in the winter when it was dark, like when it froze after a thaw and the ground became glazed with ice. But, of course, she would say, I had probably already suppressed all memory of the time I stepped out of the Moonfisher Bar, slipped and almost cracked my skull open. And she was right too. Accidents like mine were not unusual. People were slipping and sliding and banging their doped and drunken heads into things and each other in the dark; bicyclists were crashing all over the place, and there was a constant traffic of bruised bodies and broken bones to the emergency ward. All it took was a rain shower, and people were wallowing in the muck. Walking down the grimy street you would try to dodge one dead drunk and drowning human after another. And if people were not stoned out of their minds, they would probably have staring eyes just like me. Uahh, the *faces*! My wife rolled her eyes and crossed herself. Had I ever stopped to take a close look at them? If one studied them one by one, it was scary. Like they had just escaped a detox institution or closed ward or something. And this—I had to admit—was not far from the truth...

There was something to it. I did not deny it. Many of the people who had wound up in Christiania belonged to the category of social driftwood, lost souls who dreamed of escaping their past lives, kicking their self-destructive habits and making a fresh start. They came with all sorts of backgrounds. There was the respected academic whose life had been blown to smithereens when the wife left him and their four children to live with a Moldovian gypsy. There was the former politician and incorrigible drunk whose carrier derailed when his teenage daughter committed suicide. But then, there was also the Argentinian architect and grassroots activist fed up with corruption at home in Buenos Aires and charmed by the homegrown structures of the Freetown; or the American lawyer who had worked for CBS in New York but who, during an unscheduled twenty-two hour stop-over in Copenhagen, had fallen in love with a French Rastafari woman and settled with her in Christiania. Not all were lost souls. Not by any means. But it was a common ambition among the ones that were to drown in the pool of humanity and kick the bucket with a vengeance. There was the rock musician, artist, womanizer, and pusher who—half purple and half red in his swollen mug—hung out in the street outside the grocer. To the broken souls with a past, Christiania offered a reprieve in the present, a place where they could mingle with each other and the random passers by. Had they not found the spot by the Christiania grocer, most likely they would have been stuck away in psychiatric hospitals and forced to subsist on the products of the pharmaceutical industry. The Freetown was a kind of melting pot where all sorts of people merely by their physical presence in the open street were able to communicate their plight to others. With its international mix and colorful social fabric, with drunken losers on the rampage and flamboyant winners socializing directly, Christiania was a strong, nourishing and dangerous broth.

There was something to it when my wife said that you could never be sure what would happen in Christiania. *She* certainly never felt quite secure there, she said. And I said that if she depended on police patrolling the streets for security, she should examine that security more closely. Could she mention one spot on the map of Copenhagen where nothing ever happened or might happen? As for me personally, I added, I liked the feeling I had in Christiania of being protected only by my wits, awareness and mental power to read people and situations and to react. I enjoyed being on the alert. No doubt people got hurt. She was right about the Freetown being lethal when it was iced over and there were no streetlights. There *were* indeed stories of people getting hit by runaway horses. Sometimes, a dog bit a child, and you might get stabbed or hit over the head with a bottle. Sure. There *were* bar-room brawls. All it took was being in the wrong place at the wrong time. There was no way of knowing when the odd mad man would strike. You might even get burned on one of the huge bonfires that were so often blazing out in front of The Factory, if, say, the raving fire dervish hopping around with soot in his face took you for a beam or door post and threw you into the flames. Or, added my wife, you risked being raped just because you were dressed in clean clothes and did not look like something dipped in tar and rolled in a Salvation-Army clothes bin...

Or, I would remark, you risked being invited for a roll and a cup of coffee by some total strangers sitting out in front of The Cosmic Flower having their breakfast.

The problem, I think, was that my wife did not share the picture I had of myself. In her eyes, I was not so much the visionary and intrepid rebel I saw myself as being, but more like a spoiled brat whose head had been turned by naïve ideas. Just because the state authorities would like nothing better than to bulldoze Christiania, that did not mean they were by definition evil. And just because the christianites played at being NATO soldiers, or if at Christmas time, they dressed up as an army of Santa Clauses giving away merchandise to shoppers in the department stores, that didn't mean they were good by definition. Things were not black and white. A single unprejudiced glance at the Freetown, and it would be clear to anyone but me *how many* emotional cripples were in circulation out there. Psychopaths of every shape and form. If you walked down Langgade Street on a November afternoon in the drizzle, you met almost nothing but monsters. Yes, I heard right: monsters! But in the befuddled state of permanent rapture that I was in I probably only saw Santa Clauses and angels living in lovely harmony. It was enough to drive her up the wall. She ought to record me. It really was a pity I could not hear myself. When I spoke of Christiania, it was like I was drunk. And ugh... (Here my wife would pretend to shiver). When my eyes got that rapturous shine, she felt like she was going to puke. The "oh-gee-how-lovely-everything-is" look. It was all right to be enthusiastic about something, in fact that was quite charming, but it was not all right to be downright idiotic.

Sometimes, during these conversations, she got so carried away she would stick her index finger into her mouth, bend over and make rasping sounds in her throat like she was really going to puke. Oh, how wonderful it was, she would wail, the dirt and grime and junk everywhere. And oh, what wonderful demonstrations with people showing off their solidarity, Icelandic sweaters, suspenders and "clogged" feet while marching through the streets with torches in their hands chanting songs like the one about how "they" can't kill the christianites, because "they" are part christianites themselves, etc. What was that but castles in the air and a way of buying cheap indulgence? What was that but a naïve way of keeping the dream of a better world alive? Or what about those ridiculous collective meetings that I loved so much! Wasn't it just great though how the chair person was bleary eyed, had bad teeth and halitosis from smoking too much hashish? Yeah. And wasn't it great how the pushers' dogs growled and barked and got into fights?

And the way people shouted and pushed each other while herds of pea-brains sabotaged proceedings. And oh, how charming it was to listen to the lovely couple humping in the corner. Not to mention the drunken wreck wallowing in his own puke. That was *true* civilization. She could see *that*. She *really* could. Or what about that new fashion among the "artsy" women where you had to wear a boiler suit with a narrow belt glittering with cheap tinsel and tall working man's boots. It really was *very* feminine the way makeup in any form was banned from lips, eyelashes and nails because that sort of thing was counter revolutionary and bourgeois. And, oh, how could she forget the cute pusher dogs with slime and drool swinging from their mugs. With their intestines and rectums full of stinking shit. Of course, they too were very *alternative*. *Of course,* they were. I should make no mistake, she said. She really could see that. And when on top of all this, after having *seen* all of this, she happened to turn her head to the side and what did she see but the rapturous expression of her husband! Well, then...that topped it all off. No. That was *beyond* the top. That was just *too* much...

And then, the finger would go down my wife's throat, and the puking sounds would begin.

Thus spake my wife. She didn't understand me. But then who can blame me for falling for the girl in the boiler suit and the belt of cheap glitter that had sailed around the globe on a sailing ship and with her great pair of tanned legs had no problem understanding my love for the Freetown of Denmark? Once more I betrayed my wife, and once more I was caught. And that was it. Deaf to my pleadings, she packed up and left. What was supposed never to end had ended before it had really gotten started. No sooner was I free to go my own way than I longed for my chains. With nobody stopping me from going to Greece and settling I had lost all desire. I could sail across the Atlantic. I could move to Christiania. I could have affairs. I could do just about everything I had always wanted to do and had talked so much about. And I did not want to do any of it anymore. The woman who once in the dawn of our time together had listened to every word I said, who believed in me like I were the Prophet himself—this woman had overnight changed into one huge deaf ear to me. Maybe it was the time we lived in. Something in the air we breathed. What do I know? At any rate, it was around this time that Marie-Louise decided to kick Martin out. That made two of us, and because Martin had to find someplace else to live, he stumbled on the wagon belonging to Bankruptcy Benny. In short, everything seemed to conspire to make us the neighbors we were soon to become.

The morning after Martin had called, I rode my bike to Christiania. It was ten in the morning when I arrived bursting with curiosity and expectation. Marie-Louise's bicycle was nowhere to be seen near The Gunpowder House and the arched green door was closed. Walking my bike and thinking that she had probably gone to clean up and make coffee in The Poppy I passed The Gunpowder House and—there it was. Right before my eyes, neither worse nor any better than I had expected: a weather-beaten light blue caravan-wagon with paint peeling off its sides big time.

I can't tell you what I felt at that moment, if I was disappointed or pleased at the sight. What struck me more than anything was the stark reality of the thing! It seemed so utterly real it sent a shiver down my spine. Like something inevitable placed in my way, which I would have to swallow whole and digest! So what if its paint was peeling and it was in a sorry state? Was I not the same? Hadn't I also been neglected, abused and left out in the rain? So what if its metal pole was half hanging half lying abjectly on the ground? So what if its tires were flat? That just showed that nobody had had any use for it. None of it mattered. The only thing that mattered, was the feeling I had that we belonged together. I did not formulate it to myself in this way. Nevertheless, it was perfectly clear. I was the guy fated to take the wagon's pole in his hand and walk off with it...

As I stepped forth, bent down and took the metal pole in my hand, "This is it, Jack!" I told the wagon. "From now on, it's the two of us hitting the road together. You hear?"

Laura McCullough

The Elisionist

In French, when vowels are elided,
an orthographer's tool,
the apostrophe,
orchestrates with flourish,
but always
there's the choosing
between liaison or elision,
or both as in
J'arrive à l'hôtel pour une liason.
Don't tell my husband,
who speaks French, but prefers
the schwa as in amuïssement.
This is all just amuse-bouche—
to amuse the mouth—
or more correctly, amuses-bouche in the plural.
Before the hotel bed, there is the lobby,
and before the hors d'oeuvres,
something to excite the taste buds,
and a little wine, no? Or perhaps
you'd prefer to meet me
somewhere else, say the library,
where you can't buy anything,
where whatever you use is simply on loan.
We can always touch the books'
spines rather than each other's.
There's no telling what might happen.
No telling.

Laura McCullough

Meniscus:
as distinct from other planets

They told me what to expect
in this decade, but each month

it's another man asking for a kiss—
to kiss me, let's kiss—and each moon

face blooms above, behind, or across
from me as if I've seen it just

then for the first time, a wolf
in one, a bear in another, in the end,

always, just a man, but the one
this month asked, Do you fool around?

and his face was a cave begging
for a small animal to take harbor

in it, and so I was kind, but not the kind
to fool around, I told him, and went

home to my husband who splayed me
like a caught fish, bright skinned,

jumping through the meniscus of water
to air, the moon a bright-penny lure,

and he with the net, then fillets me,
my rainbow scales shedding, so our bed

is a shimmering, thin-flaked mess,
the sky above us arched by multiple

moons, and when we are done, when
my husband has knifed me clean

again, my night comes toward dawn,
and I coil into the terrestrial earth,

no longer an animal, but one
planet just looking for its sun.

Laura McCullough

The Man with Large Hands

The small loves are sometimes the best,
like falling in love with a man with large
hands because he waved them at you
across a table, his fingers splayed like

faulty dock joists, and all of a sudden
you are in a boat mooring up to one
of those skeltered poles, one foot over
the edge, trying to gain footing on

the tumbling slats, the ocean roiling
beneath you, the boat your one sure thing,
all you can depend on, yet you have one
leg hoisted like a flag of infidelity

waving in the air, and the man's hands
seem like an anchor to a part of yourself
you'd forgotten, one finger pointing
its light through the fog of your life

to the town you lived in when you
were a girl. You remember it so clearly,
there, on the other side of this big, dark
sea you crossed alone. You swore

you'd never go back, no matter what
they said to lure you, no matter how
safe you're sure it would be, these small
loves enough to slake the thirst of your

journey to this moment when one
pair of hands can suddenly break
upon you like a bucket of water
splashed against your sleeping face.

Laura McCullough

Women and the Syntactical World

Would it help to know
I'm a little in love
with your husband?

Or that I'm in love

with my own, and
I'm not going anywhere?
Or that the version of me

you hear in this poem

is a version of me
that loves mostly poets,
a few artists, one tile-guy,

and a couple of older

doctors, including
William Carlos Williams
whom a lot of women loved

and a lot of men have loved,

as well? If he—
and now I'm speaking
of your husband—loved

me, say, outside by those falls,

the one hard to find
in the city, it only
would have enlarged us both.

There is that one letter written

as a poem about cell
division as a metaphor
for communication, but my news

for you is that all poems

are love poems
in my book. Can I kiss you?
    your tongue standing

in for his tongue, your ear

delicious in its resistance.
I ask only because I want
to sidle up to the hips

of this world, bend it

over at the waist, check
the small bones of its back,
whisper into the concaves,

oh forgive me, forgive me.

I've tried to hide this,
keep my mouth closed,
but the world pried me open

long ago, and I chose not to fight

back, selecting instead,
the pleasure of giving
in to what I can't explain

and simply won't apologize for.

Duff Brenna

Cougar Lust

A Thursday morning she is at her desk trying to decide which manuscript she wants to start with. The molester one is interesting. So is the one about incest. People do what they do and her job is to polish their writing and pray for them.

When the phone rings, she picks up the receiver and says, "Harvest Home, Franny Olsen. How may I help you?"

Gruffly a voice tells her, "You got my money, lady?"

"What?" A shiver runs through her.

"You got my money?"

Franny says, "Hector?"

She hears a throaty giggle and then, "Just kidding, just kidding. This is Norman Ten Boom. Look, Franny, I'll be in your neighborhood today. How about I take you to lunch?"

"Lunch?"

"We should talk about what to do to keep that thug from ambushing you."

"Hector? Do you really think? It's been awhile. I've heard nothing."

"We both know it's a sick world, Franny. He's got his eye on you. I guarantee it. He'll show up when you least expect him."

"It's not the same world I grew up in, that's for sure, Norman. We used to say life was cheap in China. We used to pity people there. Now we pity them here." She moves her palm back and forth across her suddenly spastic colon. She can hear the Dutchman breathing the breath of waiting. "Where?" she asks.

"How about Balboa Park? The Prado. You're not far from there."

"That's thoughtful," she tells him.

"Ask anyone who knows me and they'll tell you it's one of my biggest assets, Franny. I've suffered a lot in this life. It's made me thoughtful of others." She hears him sighing. And then he says sprightly, "Twelve o'clock?"

"Twelve is fine."

"See you there."

After she hangs up, Franny whispers, "What have I done?"

———

At noon she parks in the lot closest to the Prado Restaurant. She walks past the Museum of Art and the Sculpture Garden. Hundred-foot eucalyptus and pine scrubbing the air above the Colonial Revival buildings nearby. Not far away is the San Diego Zoo. She can hear birds crying. Ahead of her is "suicide bridge" and Sixth Avenue. She turns at the Museum of Man. Climbs the stairs. Sits on a bench in front of the Old Globe Theater not far from the Bell Tower. It's a beautiful day, what the locals on TV call "another patented San Diego day"—75 degrees in mid-May, sky cloudless. Air so bright it hurts her eyes. The park's stucco buildings, Old Spanish flare, make her feel as if she has stepped into another era, the nineteenth century possibly. The grass is lush, flowers blooming with extravagant health. Swallows swift as thoughts. Sparrows squabbling. Heart thumping, nerves on edge, she stands up and paces until her arthritic feet start jabbing her again. Where is that man? Is he coming?

And you, Franny, what are you doing here waiting for that nut? Your husband may have left you, but you're still a married woman. God is watching. Watching YOU ...

"That's right. What if Harley found out?" she whispers.

When the thirty-five minute mark passes she calls it an omen, a portent. She doesn't have time for this nonsense. She has Dear Bobbi letters to read, stressed-out psyches desperate for help. That Bobbi Poe person is a fount of hope and faith for the forlorn, the lost, those despairing and Franny too. She's been working on numerous drafts of a letter she wants to send Bobbi Poe and get her advice.

74

Dear Bobbi Poe,

*After many years of numerous ailments (chronic
anemia, fibromyalgia, arthritis, gastro-enteritis and
other disgusting problems), my husband's compassion
quotient got used up and he walked out; he left me and
I can't get over the shock. So much for "in sickness and
in health"- just words anyway. Everything comes down
to actions that too often give the lie to the words we
say, don't you think, Bobbi? I believe in the Lord and
tell myself that what is happening is His plan for me,
my destiny, and I mustn't complain, just put one foot
in front of the other and keep going. But life without
my man is unbearably hard, Bobbi. I love him. We've
been married nearly thirty years and I miss him awfully.
Nights are numbingly lonely. My heart aches and I often
find myself crying. What can I do? How can I cope? I've
read your book called Calvary Witness News and found
it full of what I call hard-headed, no nonsense wisdom.
So I'm hoping you can tell me how to get over him and
move on with my life. Should I divorce him? But what
will I do without his health insurance covering me? I'm
on a diet. I exercise now. I'm trying to get well, but it's an
uphill battle. I hope you'll answer me. I am—a fifty-year-
old woman ...*

Suffering in San Diego

Franny hasn't sent the letter yet. She's not satisfied with it. She
knows there is more to say, but for the past few days words have
failed her. And now look what she's doing: waiting for a man named
Norman Ten Boom, a published poet whom she barely knows. If he
shows up, what in the world will she do with him?

She has no business acting like this ... like a desperate woman,
an eager ass waiting for her date. Is it just that she wants to get laid?

"Oh, Franny Olsen, you moron."

She makes her way back to the parking lot. A fifty-year-old fool that's what she is. Old fifty and fat and ugly and a fool. By the time she reaches her car, her sciatica has returned and she is limping. She might cry if she doesn't get a grip. When she takes her keys out, she hears a door closing behind her, a man's voice saying, "Hey, lady." Hector's primitive face flashes through her mind, his murderous eyes. *You owe me* is what she expects to hear.

Warily she turns around and sees double-chinned Norman waving. Warmth flushes through her veins like an anesthetic. The pain in her lower back vanishes. She takes off her glasses and smiles, showing him her newly whitened teeth. "I thought you weren't coming," she says. "I thought you stood me up."

He grips his head between his palms. "No, no. The traffic! Huge mess on 163."

"It's terrible how traffic is now. Everything terrible," she says. "It's a wicked world. It's murder." Her heart trips gaily. A teenage heart full of optimism.

"You look different," he says.

"Do I?"

"Off the pink?"

She blushes, remembering the pink ingénue getup she was wearing when they chanced on each other in Pisano's. "Pink isn't really my thing." She titters and he titters too. Hopeful energy is rushing through her. This *man* is flirting with *her*.

Looking Franny up and down, eyes judging her hips first, then her boob job, a wink tells her he likes what he sees. What big round eyes he has! His irises make her think of sweet brown sugar. The intensity of his stare increases until she feels she is being X-rayed.

She has dyed her hair henna red. She wears a forest green pants suit with black pumps. A petite gold cross hangs from her neck, rings on three of her fingers (the big emerald reminding her of Hector and somewhere over the rainbow). She notices Norman's powerful wrists and forearms. Hands that know their business, hands that would have taken that punk apart if he hadn't given back her ring that day he threatened her. But Norman to the rescue.

Norman the scourge of nasty muggers. Is he still at the university, still teaching poetry?

"Are you still at Cal-State?"

"Nah, I retired. Not that I wanted to. I was forced out. I'll tell you about it sometime." And then he tells her about it: "I lost my cool with those bitches running the department. It's the bear inside me what takes over and trips that anger switch. The Dutchman has to stand back when that happens. During emotional moments the bear rules. I went ballistic, Franny. Lost control. Lost perspective. The perspective that says time passes no matter what you do and people forget what seemed so important. They hung me out to dry, Franny. Threw me under the bus. That's the thanks I get. Hung me out to twist in the wind. Abandoned Norman Ten Boom. Told him to forget a full professorship. Told him to go fuck himself. I should never have left the University of Minnesota. They appreciated me there. I should've stayed. It's just the weather, the damn winter weather." Norman's voice has risen. Passersby are glancing at him and walking faster. His face is flushed. His forehead and cheeks look sunburned. His finger is shaking at her as if giving her a lecture. "Motherfuckers!" he bellows.

Then abruptly he takes a deep breath. Sighs and says, "Sorry, Franny. Excuse my French. I know women hate cussing. I apologize. I respect you, Franny, but sometimes I lose my wits over how I've been so screwed by my enemies. What a chump I let them make of me." He shakes his head, shows her his sagging profile as he stares into space and says mournfully, "I've won awards for my poetry, you know. Why don't they remember that? Who else on that faculty has been on NPR? Nobody. Just me. Just Norman Ten Boom."

Franny sees a tear trickling down his cheek. Or is it a drop of sweat? "I should have been treated better," he continues. "People should want a genius teaching their children. I was bringing big names in to do readings and lectures. For Christ's sake I got Ishmael Reed to come! It was standing room only. The newspapers were writing articles about what I was doing for the college. Did anyone appreciate it? Fuck no. They don't appreciate anything. They want you to be a cog in their wheel. I'm no cog in nobody's wheel." He wipes his eyes with the back of his hand. Takes out a hanky and blows his nose. "You know what?"

"What, Norman?"

"They took the heart out of me, Franny ... yup, tore it right out."

Her soul rushes to him. She tells herself she can save him. Nurture his poetic spirit. God would bless her for it. Behind her she hears classical music (Vivaldi? Telemann?) drifting from the restaurant and she asks, "Are you hungry, Norman?"

"I'm famished," he says. Giving her a big grin. Showing her the Dutchman again. Furious bear retreating behind the mesmerizing orbs of his beautiful eyes. "Yeah," he says, "I might have lost the battle, but I'm still gonna win the war, you'll see. Fuck em, let's eat."

———

After a small salad for her; spaghetti and meatballs for him, plus extra bread (of which he ate only the doughy centers and left the crusts) they stroll toward the botanical gardens. They stop on the footbridge, lean on the rail watching overfed koi slipping like gliding souls through watery fields of lilies. Franny chatters on and on about her strict diet, the exercise routine she adheres to. She hasn't felt this good in years. Where does all this vitality come from at her age?

"How old are you?" he says.

Blushing as she lies, she declares herself thirty-nine. "How old are you?" she asks him.

"I'll be sixty-six pretty soon."

"You don't look sixty-six."

He nods agreement. "No, I don't. People tell me I look ten years younger. I swear to God, Franny, I feel like I'm no more than eighteen. Nineteen at most. Nineteen in my heart. Nineteen in my dreams. I still have big dreams, Franny. I'm still going to the top. You watch you'll see. How do you like my hair? I dyed it, can you tell? Does it look natural?"

His hair is sandy brown now. "I liked the white mane you had, Norman. You looked very distinguished with white hair. It made you look like a noble lion."

"I'm not a lion now? I don't look distinguished?"

"Yes, but not quite in the same way."

"People tell me I have a youthful glow. I tell you I'm only *nineteen*." He taps his heart. "In here." Closing his eyes a moment, he smiles as if imagining himself at nineteen. Then he pulls a pack of smokes from his pocket and offers her one. She hesitates. Then takes it. Lights up. Doesn't inhale.

"My only vice," he says. "Mainly when I get nervous. You make me nervous, but it's a good nervous. I'm glad to feel nervous. It makes me feel more alive. Thanks for coming, Franny. You don't know how much this means to me. My wife and I don't get along. We're sleeping in separate rooms now. I get so lonely. I've got my son, but I hardly ever see him. He lives with his mother in Minneapolis. You don't have any kids, do you, Franny?"

She likes how he talks so rapidly, like a ventriloquist scarcely moving his heavy lips. His face is old and tough. Picked on by the system. Who isn't? Oh dear, oh dear. Poor man. Franny wants to help him. Tell him: Franny is here. Everything will be all right, dear. Trust in Franny and the Lord, the light of the world. *He that followeth me shall not walk in darkness, but shall have the light of life.* Franny hugs herself, covers her agitation with another pull on her cigarette, another expulsion of smoke. She has forgotten how good cigarettes can smell. And pipes too. Harley had smoked a pipe when he was in college, until someone told him he looked like a cliché.

Touching Norman's hand briefly she says, "No, I don't have kids. Wish I did. But Harley and I quit trying. He said he didn't want to bring kids into such a horrible world."

"He's right," agrees Norman. "Ain't doing em no fuckin favor. Just look around. This planet is full of monsters. You got a gun, Franny? You got double-lock deadbolts on your doors? You got a security system?"

Franny wags her head no.

"That thug Hector mugging you."

"I offered the emerald to appease him, Norman."

"Out there preying on helpless ladies. He almost got you. If I hadn't been there I hate to think what would'a happened. For sure he would have kept your emerald. Maybe taken all them." Norman points to the jewelry adorning her fingers. "Maybe take you in the alley and do some things. Fucking animal."

"Hector," she says in a timid whisper, Hector's dark eyes menacing her, his handsome face filling her with shameful hunger to be a wild thing again in her life. "I didn't tell you I dented his car. I thought I was doing the right thing giving him the ring. I had no idea the car was stolen. The emerald was a down payment. He seemed like a nice boy, Norman." She pauses a second. Then adds: "No he didn't. He wasn't nice at all. He was scary." She pauses to reflect. And then adds, "Killer written all over him."

"Killer written all over him is right, Franny. I was in the right place at the right time. It happens to me a lot. It's the instinct in me. I wasn't going to get a torpedo that day, but the bear wanted one. I had no choice but to go in Pisano's and order the bear a torpedo and get me a beer. It's mystical how things happen to me. I'm mystical. I'm a mystery to myself, Franny. But I know this: that thug would have ripped you off if I hadn't been where the bear wanted to be that day. Listen, we need to get you prepared. We'll get you a handgun. I hate guns, but the way things work in this godforsaken country you're a damn ostrich if you don't have firepower. The biggest, meanest man in the world is no match for a gun." He pauses, narrows his eyes and continues. "What you really need is a man like me to protect you. You get me angry I can be your worst nightmare." Norman's fists swipe the air. "I was a hell of a street-fighter," he says, "back in Philly when I was a kid."

Franny is wondering how she looks in such direct light. Are her crow's feet showing through the heavy makeup? She turns toward the gardens, the huge lath structure full of tropical plants and trees and shade. He follows her while they slip inside, into cool green paradise. Stroll along narrow pathways lined with leaves so large she feels they could swallow her. She wonders if he will kiss her. The thought makes her panic and she starts chatting about how beautiful the gardens are, how they make her feel as if she has somehow been transported to South America, the equator, the Congo. She bends over and smells a white orchid, its musk saturating her senses, making her wish for proms, chiffon, tuxedos, romantic music, twinkling stars, a full moon, the back seat of a Chevy. She wonders if he is staring at the slimmed down roll of her rump. She glances back and sees him sitting on a bench toeing the stub of his cigarette.

"I guess I better get back to work," she says.

"Do me a favor," he says.

"A favor?"

"Just stand in that sunbeam a minute. Let me see what happens." From his shirt pocket he takes out pad and pen and starts writing. In a minute, he looks up and says, *"Light beaming through lath squares brightens her breasts. Elephant leaves dip their eager ears towards her mellifluous voice. The veins in the leaves are heartstrings hoping to enfold her. My words beckon. Look at her, the light of my life is listening."*

Franny blinks rapidly. Her breath quickens. "You just sat there and wrote that?"

"For you. When I looked up and saw you," his arms making an inclusive gesture, taking in the botanical scene, "the words flew into my Ursa Major eyes. Inspiration. I haven't been inspired in a long time. Thank you, Franny. Thanks much, light of my life."

"I feel dizzy," she says. "No one ever wrote me a poem before."

"Harley never wrote you poetry? Didn't you tell me he was a writer?"

"A wannabe."

"Ah yes, too many of those around cluttering up slush piles. They get in the way of the good stuff."

She sits on the bench next to him and fans her face with her hand while saying. "Harley never even bought me a Valentine. He's about as unromantic as they come. At least with me. Maybe with his latest lover he's different. She might insist that theirs is a great romance, don't you think?"

"She's probably an egocentric idealist," says Norman. "She's probably a selfish romantic like all romantics are. They're the kind who steal husbands. But I have to admit it, I'm a little bit like that too, Franny. A romantic. An idealist." His knee is pressing her knee. "Franny, look here, let's not be a pair of coots. We're too old to waste time. I feel you feel what I feel. Am I right, my darling? Have we found each other again after all these years? What we'll do about it is the question. You want to go to a motel, or shall we go to your house and find out how serious this is?"

The bluntness of his approach makes her unable to catch a breath. Her mind whirls. She's incoherent. She wants him. She wants him to go away. He's married. Oh dear, oh dear. *Adultery*.

"Your wife," she says.

"We keep separate rooms. She's got her life and I've got mine."

Franny looks at the pathway between the botanical splendors and says, "You know, I still live in the same house I shared with Harley. It's too big for me, Norman. I've decided to rent the extra bedrooms. I have rooms to rent, Norman. Would you like to take a look and consider renting one from me? They're all reasonable, very comfortable. I had an ad in the paper, but no one answered."

"Right now?" he says.

She looks at her watch. "I'm a little late already, but okay."

"Let's go in my car. We'll come back for yours later."

She calls her boss and tells him she is sick and on her way to the doctor's. It must be something she ate for lunch. She will be back later, or if she can't come back she promises to work overtime tomorrow and not charge Harvest Home for it.

"What are you working on?" asks her boss.

She looks at Norman Ten Boom and says, "I picked it out of the slush pile. Mainly because of the title. It's a study, interviews about older women seducing younger men. It's called *Cougar Lust*."

"How younger?"

"Some are much younger. Like thirty years."

"The women aren't school teachers are they? That stuff has worn out its welcome."

"No, they're from all walks of life. A lot of them are married."

"Sounds good. Pass it on if it holds up."

In her mind she starts composing the manuscript. Giving an imagined chapter a weave so no one can connect her with it, with her life. She remembers a letter she read in Bobbi Poe's book:

Dear Bobbi:
I am fifty years old and have fallen in love with a younger man. Actually, he's hardly more than a boy. He's only nineteen, Bobbi. I'm ashamed, but I can't help myself. He's so ...

As they drive in Norman's car to Franny's house in Kensington, she tries to make sense of what she's doing. But she can't. This vigorous old man whose voice belongs in an opera has moved her in ways no one has moved her before—not even her husband. She tugs at her skirt, but it refuses to be ruled. Full of fire, the fabric clings to her, outlining her thighs and the hollow between them, where she hasn't been touched since long before her husband left her.

Dear Can't Help Herself:
What you are doing is damned by a social order
that continually wars with itself over the meaning of
Scripture. But be that as it may, the Bible still contains
the answers you need. Your personal relationship with
God is paramount. Your understanding of His Word
is more important than any interpretations held by
innumerable theologians. Forget them. Flip to any page
and you will find in code the path of truth and light
and the bounties of love. Get on that path and follow
wherever it leads you. If it leads to the arms of this boy,
then so be it. God has sent him unto thee for a purpose.

Maybe you are meant to save him or he is there to save you. Listen to the urgings of your immortal soul. As long as you love God, you won't do anything wrong, anything sinful or reeking of brimstone. Memorize the following lines and when you have doubts soothe yourself by saying over and over: "I came that you may enjoy life, and have it in abundance, until it overflows ... There is no fear in love; for perfect love casts out fear."

Faithfully yours ...

Glancing at Norman, she sees him staring straight ahead, his gaze so visionary it's as if he knows the future. It occurs to her that God is wonderfully mysterious in the way his wonders unfold. Just when you think your life is over, he sends you something new and exciting. He sends you a Dutchman bear named Norman Ten Boom. He sends you a new pair of eyes and a poem. A security system. A gun. He sends you a warning that you need double-lock deadbolts for your doors.

Roisin McLean

Cleavage

Five minutes late for Geoff's reading at Fowey River U., you stride your black suede heels into Lostwithiel Library past the chevron-bricked lobby to the sunny Arbor Room, where you spot him up front, chatting with three young female students. His hair glints more silver than a year ago. He's rolled up the sleeves of his black shirt with teal pinstripes in a rugged, sexy way. You do not love him.

Unable to manage eye contact yet, you thank the gods that his back is to you. But his back is to you, which sends up a red flag; he usually faces the door to gauge the scene. Your cheeks flame scarlet over his for-fun-only flirtatious emails and your liquor-soaked responses—keystrokes with no sense of propriety: "Let me drink from you; be my sustenance." Your clothes and dignity turn to glass. If he turns, his baby blues will see you nude.

You hide in the back row, and your sexy black pencil skirt rides too short up your thighs. You cross your legs and shift your bottom. Better—although a blue-haired lady in polyester stares up your muscled calves to your fitted silk blouse, to your feathered hair, meets your eyes, looks away.

During the eloquent introduction, which you know by heart, your eyes drift from the faux marble tile floor to soundproofing tiles in the ceiling—twelve across by twenty deep—to young potted yews casting shadows on a mural of firs. Strange—no dust motes in this late afternoon sun. Geoff strides on applause to the podium. You center yourself on the back of a broad navy blazer, study the frayed end of a scarf casually slung over the shoulder. Geoff's voice, quavering—a first—washes through the room. You send him lapis-lazuli blue light to calm his nerves. Clutched on your lap is his book, which you've read twice already. You float, cradled, on the rhythmic waves of his words.

85

He can*not* be reading the scene about the conference five years ago. Your torso twitches. From twenty feet away, he reaches right through that massive woman you're hiding behind and pokes you square in the chest. Reaches through time itself to that very conference, when you won a raffle to meet with a famous author. A singular conference during which, on the penultimate day, you sat, hands in your lap, at an antique table in a room with books shelved from floor to ceiling. The hypnotizing aromas of old paper, the glue in case bindings, Geoff's wool overcoat, his nasty chest cold. His hands paging through your short story manuscript, his right index finger pausing here and there, touching your words. As you listened to his mesmerizing voice, his kind comments, and astute proposed changes, something unworldly, psychic, possessed you— forced you to feel an invisible cord binding your sternum to his, which ruffled your passions, flustered your senses. Observing your sudden fidgeting, he finished quickly, asked if you had questions. You said no, thanked him, and fled. Pondered the strange feeling for days. Wondered if you were lovers in a previous life. Dismissed it entirely as a strange symptom of jet lag or an eruption from the Muse of creative joie de vivre. Joined a master's program, were astonished to find him on the faculty there. As if it were all meant to be. But what *all*, what *be*? All too silly for credibility, you think. And yet—

"... synchronicity." Geoff's voice lingers on the word to signal the end of the passage, which is clearly the end of the passage, but he is an experienced reader and empathizes with his audience, with humanity. Applause ends your reverie.

As you join the long, languid flow toward his thick black autograph, someone behind you shrieks "Mekka." It's Dona, a former classmate, a petite poet with jet-black hair in a stylish wedge, whom you haven't seen since you both graduated last year, the oldest two in a class of intergenerational students.

"*Look* at you!" Dona says.

"There are fringe benefits to divorce," you respond, stooping to hug her, remembering with pleasure her earth-mother embrace.

"I'm *sorry*," she says.

"I'm not," you say.

"Which explains your relieved and happy glow," Dona says. Her smiling eyes roam your face, pleased for you.

With lowered voice, you tell her that last year was a year from hell, the year you divorced your lying husband and suffered anorexia, inordinate fear, night after month of little sleep, and the suicidal rock bottom of the Betrayal Trench, a regular Bermuda Triangle where you longed for oblivion. Instead, into that maelstrom of agita and angst, up popped Geoff's email in your lonely inbox. You don't tell Dona about him but wish that you could. That he lived too far away, Vancouver, for in-person get-togethers, but he drank merlot and chatted online with you throughout the day, many nights, and you found self-preservation and the courage to rise, exercise, lift weights, three pounds to five pounds to eight, dream of springtime and sex. He was a good and kind friend to hold your hand figuratively through the typhoon of emotions, which he was weathering himself, still devastated by his partner's betrayal and split. You held his hand in return, and he somehow surged into your heart like "YOU'VE GOT MALE" along with a flood of libido in your nether regions—hardly part of any rational plan, but your heart and hormones didn't ask your brain first.

The autograph line moves up. You greet the man joining Dona, the always-smiling poetry professor, his beard and tweed jacket of complementary silvers and grays. A student interrupts, and you can't focus on his multisyllabics over snippets of Dona's conversation now behind you: "never seen such a transformation ... looks like Marilyn Monroe." Gross hyperbole, but you smile and stand straighter, gut and butt tucked in—shades of Miss Georgianna's charm class way back in sixth grade.

"Should I address this to you or someone else?" Geoff asks, not smiling, reaching for his book in your hands.

Too late to run. You swallow your tongue and point to your chest, are not sure then if he recognizes your more-svelte self. He's flushed as he writes "To Mekka" with great flourish. Is he ill? Your eyes trace the familiar G as he signs: Geoffrey. Not his customary autograph. Formal, far away. Your breast touches his bicep. You jump back, regain proper territorial distance. As distant in time as Chaucer, for whom Geoff's parents had named him.

"Did you miss the reading?" he asks, still not smiling. Which is when you suspect that *you screwed up*—maybe he wanted, needed, to see you, greet you, *before* he read. Or maybe you've spun an intricate web of self-lies to trick your mind into playing masochistic games with your passionate desire for a partner you can trust. Your explanation of rush-hour traffic sinks into mumble, and you step aside. So that's that. Dream dreamt. Reality sucks. What could you have been thinking?

Outside in oddly warm March air, you fish for your keys, too confused to cry.

"Mekka." It's Dona. "The department will go out after—want to come?"

Back inside—you resist looking at Geoff—Dona updates you on her chapbook prep, then segues into the phenomenon of conversing with lesbians about the beauty of women, which is not a discussion, she says, men can have with men. You venture it's sociocultural and don't ask if she's suddenly switched sides of the fence. Then she's on to other tip-of-the-iceberg comments until Geoff and stragglers meander toward the door. Geoff doesn't look at you.

Outside in front of the gang, he says, "Mekka, I like your blouse." You could have intrigued with the name of its color, Aegean Sea Blue, been glib and gay, but *no*, your eyes drop involuntarily as you whisper thanks and blush. You look up to see Geoff crimson but beaming. Too big a smile? Is he laughing at your awkwardness? He wouldn't do such a thing—would he? Would you? Has anyone noticed your adolescent exchange?

At Rendezvous, a restaurant/bar in a converted railway station, complete with three-ton chandelier and stained-glass windows, you set your purse on a stool at Geoff's high table, chat with his friend, the smiling bearded professor, and drink a vodka on the rocks like it's iced tea in August because Geoff, king of the mixed message, once again won't look at you. You float to another table and, with Dona, stroke current students suffering lack of confidence. Share their fried calamari and memories of summer residencies in Rome. Promise to attend their graduation. Write their names on a napkin because you won't remember. Back at Geoff's table, you order another vod. It tastes weaker than the first, so you drink it fast, too. You can't look at Geoff. You watch the piano player, who checks you out to and from the restroom. Nice, to be acknowledged, even like that sometimes.

"Mekka." Your questioning eyes, swimming in molecules of music pooled and reflected on the glossy black piano, catch up with your turning head, and you are looking into Geoff, who is looking into you and smiling in shadow. Who turned out the light over the table? Where did everyone go? He smiles so big, his eyes squeeze closed. You smile back in kind. Two people smiling at each other, blind. You ease up on your smile so you can see. So has he. He raises his glass to toast. You have only ice in your glass. Does a toast count if there's nothing to drink? You clink glasses in silence. You try to drink melt from the bottom of your glass. There is none. Your mouth says, "I tried," your shoulders shrug, and your head turns back to the piano. You *tried*? Tried to what? Tried to let your sabotaging other-self scare him away? Your realize you're so shit-faced—on *only* two vodkas—you're lost between psychological observer and participant, between twit and "intelligent person with advanced degree." What, now you're schizo? You're too old for this crap.

The light returns. You help the smiling, bearded professor count the gang's collected currency, which is cracked because you're crocked and he's been drinking Perrier. People rise. Stool legs scrape.

Geoff opens his arms for a hug and says, motioning to your blouse, "To a silk day. It is silk, isn't it?" WTF? Your brain can't form the words that your mouth can't produce. His smile crinkles his eyes closed again. Good thing—you'll lose yourself in them this close.

You lean in to hug, barely touch, no mixed message there. You can't look back—a year must pass before you'll see him next—and you manage not to tumble down the steps when your right heel slips. The car drives itself home—guardian angels at work. You won't test them like that again. You try to look ahead, but the future yawns with boredom.

Four days later, he emails from Paris. You look fantastic, he writes. You perk up, but you won't hear from him for three weeks now while he's on tour in Europe, a different city or country every day or two. You brace for Geoff withdrawal. Plan A: Set your sights on the year-long horizon and roll with the waves, one day at a time. Plan B: Don't ever email him again; it's just an infatuation, or infantile desire, and it's over—or should be. Plan C: Try navigating the "land-ho," lounge-lizard route. Plan D: You're not a whore, so scratch Plan C and instead seek a shrink, one who's expert on hypomania, transference, and rebound relationships. Plan E: Scratch Plan D, and instead Google postmenopausal testosterone + intense sexual desire. Which it turns out is rare, but you've got it, per the blood test, but only for Geoff, who's older than you, so you're not a cougar, but that's no consolation.

The best is yet to come, Geoff always says. To pass time between work, the gym, you drink absinthe at home, surf BsideU. com, and study self-help manuals, which define infatuation as three months long. Odd—you've been infatuated with Geoff for a year. Maybe three if you were in denial the first two. Why do the emails feel so real, the fleeting moments of real him, in person, a dream shimmering in mist? Is it the L word, wrapped up in a bow of delusion? You shiver, sip more absinthe, recall his flushed smile, wear it like dew. Wear it like the mirrored last image adrift in his eyes: fitted blouse—silk—Aegean Sea blue. Patient blue. True blue. More like hungry-loins you or "fifty-five going on sixteen" you. This is not normal. You weren't always shallow, not to diminish Geoff's virtues. Have you always been hormonally challenged? No. So how can you teach your heart that desire isn't love? Is it even possible now—old dogs, new tricks, and such? Back to square one.

With legs up on the sofa, new dog at your feet, and Augustine Pinot Noir in a crystal goblet this season, you and Geoff are still exchanging emails but less frequently and with no hint of flirtation. Your emotions have calmed. Stable is nice. And then he sends a summer photo, you can't take your eyes off his bulging biceps, and you send a photo back, a low-cut tank with skirtini, which you always wear around the house. He messages three times, commenting on your "worthy cleavage." And up pops your libido—creaming your panties like you're a teenager again every time his name pops up bold in your inbox.

The Pinot Noir is smooth, no tannins. You pour another glass. You reflect on the relationship, how the titillating highs of your roller-coaster emotions gave you vertigo, how his mood swings sent you around the bend, how your mood swings flummoxed him—all via email. You decide, calmly and maturely, that someone must close this amusement-park ride: either care for him enough to spare him you, or care for yourself enough to spare you him. No other options sail into view, other than keep loving this man however he wishes, so you choose to sleep on it but second-guess yourself and suspect procrastination. Then you third-guess yourself and wonder if he, perhaps infatuated with you but still shy, is thinking the same thing.

"Mekka," you say to yourself, "you're fifty-six—grow up."

You raise your goblet in the direction of Vancouver, toast this mesmerizing man who's been lighting your world, and bid a silent and caring adieu to what surely must be lunacy. You take another sip, drain the goblet, and cry until tears drip off your chin, tickle down your cleavage, your sternum. Which is when you start laughing. Sure, adieu, for six hours until you change your mind again—could be six minutes this time. Or six seconds even, which, in fact, is how long it takes you to start daydreaming about seeing him in March at Fowey River U., when you will probably again wear that fitted silk blouse, Aegean Sea blue, with an extra button, maybe two, undone. What's wrong, really, with a little cleavage between friends?

Rick Mulkey

Hummingbird

Imagine each liqueur-soaked rose as a potential love affair
on this capricious tour of blossom-scented air.

Wings in constant flight, he reveals himself
as stained glass let loose to glaze summer air.

He lives in the moments between inhale
and exhale, between hawk-shadow and sun-laced air.

Imagine the stamen encased in a drop of rain, carnal thrum
of wind in poplars whispering to the pollen stained air,

we all fail love. Watch how easily he turns from rose to
    heather,
the way, as children, we'd practice our flying from the top
    stair,

choosing opportunity over safety, flapping our arms
    desperately,
believing we could abandon our solid selves, hover as light
    and air.

Rick Mulkey

Desire

This is not light to wake in; this is August light, wind-borne
and sun-leached, light to worry down to its smallest
    exhalations.
From her hospital bed, she can see sunlight wrench the
    scorched limbs
of the marlberry beyond the window. She knows well these
    betrayals,

exposures to pain, the drainage tube in her chest, the nurse's
    knotted hands
rooting through meat, scraping across breastplate. Another
    morning
this moan might mean desire, a lover's hand brushing
    nipple, kissing that
bulb which will become the wintry bloom of what once was
    human.

Rick Mulkey

In the Strip Clubs of Bluefield, West Virginia

No one's fool enough here to call them
Gentlemen's Clubs. No need for euphemism.
Weeknights they're crammed with ex-miners
and railroad men smoking Salems
and drinking Pabst Blue Ribbon in a can.
Most haven't mined since '80 when they voted Reagan.
They'd rather drink than vote again, figuring
chances are better playing the lottery's scratch & win.

The women are beautiful when the lights
are dim and smoke thick as valley fog.
One brunette who dances every night is scarred,
gray seam from hip to tit. It's hard not to want
to touch it. She whispers in an ear,
"Dig long and hard enough, my daddy
always said, and you'll turn up diamonds."
Still you could find love here, of a certain kind.

Walking beyond the rail yard, Victorian homes
of scrolled gingerbread decay to shades of gray.
Only the cemeteries are manicured, graves smooth
as billiard felt. That's why men arrive early
Wednesday nights. Dollars unfolded as if promised
for Baptist collection plates. Every sinner hoping
for a little extra. Why shouldn't they go down
on their knees, pray for any life beyond this one.

Rick Mulkey

September

September is the syntax of pick and shovel
in the Tazewell quarry of my youth, the auger
burrowed out of sight, money in a young man's pocket,
and after work, the honking horn at the gate.
It is the homecoming queen rising slowly
from her backyard swing, knowing she'll make him wait.
It is the distraction of rain in the middle of the night,
and the moth's jazzy susurration beneath a porch light.
It is the fragrance of girls fashioned into women,
the smell of late night love in a Dodge,
the bittersweet blooming of dawns
that always arrive, and how sunlight those mornings
is the one grief we never forget.

Victor Rangel-Ribeiro

A Single Object of Singular Desire

Goa, Portuguese India, 1933

When Mottu the village postman in Tivolem heard that Marie-Santana had at last returned to her grandmother Angelinh' Granny's house next door after a prolonged absence overseas, his thoughts flew to that last evening they had spent playing together on the nearby hilltop, all of twenty years ago, he already thirteen and she a year younger. As a fresh breeze blew in from the west and they watched the sun dip molten gold into a shimmering Arabian Sea, he had taken her hand in his and told her, teary eyed and anguished, that he did not want her to leave, that he loved her. He had expected to kiss her then, as he had seen grown-ups do when they thought no one was watching, but instead she had turned just as he leaned forward, and run down the hill, leaving him to follow after, kicking at stones all the way.

Now he asked his wife what Marie-Santana's husband was like, and Annabel told him that Marie-Santana had returned by ship alone, that she had never married.

He seemed troubled by the news. "Then we must find her a husband soon," he said. "She'll never find a husband on her own; she's an old maid already."

Mottu's concern over his neighbor's unmarried state became more acute when Annabel told him a week later that Marie-Santana had refused to meet a prospective suitor he had recommended. The man was a cousin of his, a clerk in a government office, and therefore assured of a steady if not overly lucrative employment for life. Being parsimonious, he had even saved up a tidy sum of money. Yet Marie-Santana had refused to consider him.

"What does Mar'-Santan' have against him?" Mottu asked. "That he's a little deaf in one ear? People get that way in their fifties. That he's bald? That happens, too."

"It's not him," Annabel said. "She won't consider anybody. No matter who."

To Mottu, this was bad news. It proved to him that his instincts had been right—Marie-Santana had remained single because, even though she had run away after that aborted kiss, she was in love with him, so much in love that now she would not consider any other man, would accept no substitute. As he thought about this, he suddenly realized its true significance—he had gone through life underrating himself. Here was proof, if proof were needed, that he was desirable. Not just his wife, but another woman—a woman who had been overseas, and no doubt had had her pick of suitors— another woman loved him. He looked in the mirror again, as he had done when first Annabel had told him that Marie-Santana had returned unwed. He stuck out his chin and moved his jaw from side to side and narrowed his eyes. Once again the mirror did not lie: he was truly handsome. He decided he would look even better if he grew a mustache.

That night, when Annabel joined him in bed, she was surprised by the urgency of his lovemaking. When they had finished he did not fall asleep as he usually did. Instead, he caressed her, and she snuggled up against him. In the warmth of their closeness he began to think of that other being who lived directly across the lane, just a few paces away, yet was no doubt tossing forlornly on her bed. He contrasted his own situation with hers. Annabel and he were comfortable with each other; no fireworks in their lovemaking, but deep comfort. At any hour of the night, if he turned, she turned. And if she turned, he turned as well. It was a spontaneous response. Who could Marie-Santana turn to? A pillow? He wondered what it would feel like to make love to her, who had been alone for so long. On the one hand, she might be all afire; on the other, she might be like ice.

Between fire and ice, Motto now decided that Marie-Santana was a combination of the two—a volcano, gone cold. That could explain why, in all these weeks since her return, she had not pursued him, as he had feared she would. Either way, he might have to teach her to make love, from having been so long alone. He thought again of how she had wasted all those years, saving herself for him. A tragedy! And now, even with a proposal from a good man, a man of means though bald and a little deaf, she was still waiting—for what? For him, Mottu, to leave Annabel? For Annabel to die? Lying as he now was beside his sleeping wife, he realized—although theirs had been an arranged marriage—that he did not want Annabel to die. That aside, Marie-Santana would be in for an extremely long wait, for Annabel was as healthy as a—a—but whatever animal he thought of as healthy, whether cow, water buffalo or tiger, or even his son Little Arnold's pet turtle, he immediately saw that animal wasting away and dying, sometimes from unnatural causes. The possibility of Annabel's death now became more real. He remembered a cousin who had been widowed in his twenties. Why should his own marriage be immune? Shuddering, he began to imagine a life without Annabel, a desolate life, a barren life, filled with loneliness, their six-year-old son left motherless. Mottu's face contorted, his eyes began to fill with tears even as he pictured himself weeping. He saw himself being comforted by caring neighbors, but most of all by Marie-Santana, ministering to him day and night. Although she did this willingly and untiringly, her face was a mask, and he saw at once that he had been right, she would have to be taught the art of love, step by step. He lingered over each step, deliciously, until she, now an expert, was providing him with endless hours of connubial bliss.

"Day and night," he said, half-aloud. "Isn't that amazing!"

"Isn't what amazing?" Annabel asked, stirring sleepily by his side.

"That's amazing," he said hastily, not knowing what else to say. "I was dreaming."

She threw a comforting arm around him and once again drifted off to sleep.

Mottu, however, found sleep evading him. His wife's trusting touch had shamed and humbled him; he became aware that he had committed a grievous sin against her, if only in his mind. Now that he thought about it, he had committed a whole series of sins in his mind, he a married man, against her and against God and His sacrament of marriage, in the lustful way he had pictured himself and Marie-Santana tumbling about. Tumbling and rolling. All that wild moaning! And in recollecting it he was sinning yet once again. This was March, this was Lent, the middle of Lent, when the vicar in all his sermons was calling attention to sin and the need for contrition and repentance. And he, Mottu, had committed adultery, had even killed off his wife. In his mind, true, but had the vicar not said, impure and sinful thoughts were often worse than deeds? With Easter around the corner, he would be expected to go to Communion. To receive Communion, he would have to go to confession. That meant having to confess to the vicar or to the curate, and though a carved wooden screen would shield him from being wholly seen by the priests, either of them would recognize his voice. They always did, he knew, even though they gave not a hint of it when assigning penance: three Our Fathers and three Hail Marys, and three Glory be to the Father, the Son, and the Holy Ghost. This was the penance imposed on him most often because, in the past, all his sins had been venial. What would they assign him now, loaded down as he was with mortal sin?

At last the solution came to him: he would simply receive Communion without going to confession; each priest would think he had confessed to the other. "Thank you, Lord," he cried inwardly, ecstatic. But then he felt, not God's grace, but God's frown: Instantly the thought of receiving Communion while not in a state of grace appalled him; he would be adding a far more grievous sin to those he had already committed, so grievous that for that alone he could fry in Hell. Had the Devil gotten him already? He crossed himself as well as he could with his left hand, because his right was pinned under Annabel.

No sooner had he crossed himself than a far better solution suggested itself—he did not need to go to the vicar at all, nor even to the curate. All he had to do was walk over the north hill to

Goregaon, a very long and tiring walk up its steep and unforgiving slopes, to be sure, but there at the end of it he would find a most welcome sight—the centuries-old Church of Saint Martha of the Miracles, where the vicar was so new, and so old, and so troubled by cataracts that he could not recognize his own parishioners, let alone a stranger making the long trek from Tivolem.

Following the sage counsel given him by the vicar of St Martha's, Mottu now began avoiding the source of his temptation, and found some mental peace. "Is Mottu all right?" Marie-Santana asked Annabel. "I haven't seen him in the longest time."

"His work keeps him busy," Annabel replied. "I'll tell him you asked."

Days later Marie-Santana, setting out as usual for her weekly trip to the Friday bazaar in Mapusa, had walked halfway down the long and palm-fringed road to town when she spied a cyclist riding somewhat erratically towards her. Happy to see it was Mottu, she waved; he waved back enthusiastically, letting go of the handlebars, and as the bike veered to one side, she held her breath.

"You've still got a long way to walk, Mar'-Santan'," he said. "I'll give you a ride. Come, climb on to the crossbar."

"Thanks, Mottu, but it's pleasant and I'd rather walk," she said, as he stopped alongside. "Besides, I see you've already been to Mapusa. Why should you go back again?" Her suspicions were aroused; she could smell liquor on his breath.

He made a face. "I've not been to Mapusa yet," he said. "I've been riding up and down here for half an hour, waiting for you to show up. And now you disappoint me?"

"Waiting for me?" she said, surprised. "Did Annabel send you, then, with a message?"

"Yes," he said, then added, somewhat sheepishly, "that is, no. You're Annabel's friend; I just thought I'd spare you a tiring walk."

"Mottu, what's come over you? You're a married man. What would people say?"

He had stopped in the middle of the narrow road, with one

foot on the ground. Now, with a bus approaching, they moved to one side.

The bus whooshed by.

"And what would people say?" he asked.

She put a hand to nose and mouth and waited for the dust to settle, then briskly resumed her walk, anxious to get away from him; he turned his bike around and rode unsteadily beside her.

"I'll tell them the truth," he said.

"The truth!" Her uneasiness increased. "And what would that be?"

"That you love me," he said.

"Mottu, are you crazy?"

"Don't call me crazy," he said. "A little drunk, maybe. But crazy, not me! You love me, but are afraid to admit it." He leaned a hand on her shoulder.

"Take your hand off me," she snapped, slapping at his wrist.

He leaned even harder. "Mar'-Santan', I'm going to do what I should have done the day you came back. I'm going to kiss you."

She backed away and he lost his balance, so he had to plant a foot on the ground once again.

"Shame on you!" she cried. "Think of Annabel."

"You told Annabel you missed seeing me. I have missed seeing you too." His face puckered. "I don't want to think of Annabel," he said.

She watched him with disgust.

"Come closer, Mar'-Santan', love," he pleaded. "Annabel's not here to see us. Come, just one little hug and a kiss."

A rage seized her. As he leaned into her again, she grabbed hold of the back of the saddle and pushed with all her might. The bike went off at an angle; she watched him teeter at the edge of the road, and the next moment he and the bike had fallen into the field below. It was a four-foot drop and Marie-Santana became concerned. She ran to the spot to find him sitting, shaken but unharmed, on the soft and sandy ground.

"Are you all right?" she called.

He picked himself up without answering.

"We've been friends since childhood," she said. "You are a married man, and your wife is my friend. Must you spoil everything now, for all of us?"

"I'm ashamed," he said. "And sorry." He was weeping now. "If you tell Annabel, I'll die. She's a good woman; don't hurt her, Mar'-Santan'!"

"This madness has to stop," she said curtly. "Go home, Mottu!" And she set off again towards town.

"Don't tell, please don't tell, Mar'-Santan'!" He was back on the deserted road, his voice carrying on the wind. "Annabel, my wife! Forgive me, my Annabel!"

By the middle of June the monsoon struck Goa in all its demonic fury, and by June 23, just before St. John the Baptist's Day, Angelinh' Granny's well had filled to within six feet of the brim. The water looked cool and inviting, and Marie-Santana decided to jump in and swim, having first checked that old jutting stones still provided a foothold, and crevices serving as handholds would help her clamber out.

"You swim faster than my turtle, Mar'-Santan' Aunty," a child's voice cried out, and she looked up, startled to see Little Arnold peering over the parapet. "Tomorrow, when I come with Daddy and the other men, and we all jump in, will you teach me to swim?"

They came in a boisterous group, singing raucous songs in honor of the saint, and to each of them Angelinh' Granny gave a tot of cashew *feni.* By the time the bottle was half-empty Forttu the tavern-keeper had jumped on to the parapet, pinched his nose shut, and leapt into the water, followed by Govind and Kashinath and Braganza the postmaster, with Mottu the last to jump. The square well was barely fifteen feet across, but Mottu was a weak swimmer, and the water was forty feet deep; having dared to jump in, he panicked on surfacing, and immediately made his way to the side, spewing water out of both sides of his mouth like a ship steaming into Panjim harbor. He found a crevice and clung to it, content to watch newcomers jump in one after the other.

Standing on the wet parapet and about to jump in, Little Arnold had watched his father thrashing about in the water, seen the panic in his eyes, and found the sight less than reassuring. If his father was having so much trouble down there, after all those years of holding his nose and jumping in feet first, what was the point of jumping in when one did not know to swim at all, and needed to have dried coconuts tied at one's back to keep from drowning?

"I'll hold your hand," Marie-Santana said, climbing up beside him, and Josephine Aunty the gossip drew in a sharp breath of disapproval because Marie-Santana should not be jumping into that well at all, not with all those married men down there just waiting to see her skirt go ballooning over her head. But Little Arnold backed off, even though he wanted Marie-Santana to teach him to swim.

Marie-Santana jumped just as Forttu was climbing out. Mottu was chagrined; he had avoided her since the incident on the Mapusa road, yet here she was, in the well with him, and no way for him to escape but to climb out in a hurry, drawing attention and losing face. The other swimmers stayed to the side until she surfaced; seeing Forttu preparing to jump in again, she too got out of the way, quietly treading water. Though she was facing away from Mottu, he was sure she had seen him in the shadows.

Forttu stood right next to Little Arnold. "Come on, let's both jump," he said, and Little Arnold wanted to right then, his heart said jump but his knees said no, and his feet pulled him back from the brink.

"Pinch your nose shut!" Forttu said, and the child did, and the next thing he knew Forttu had picked him up with a hand beneath each armpit and tossed him right in the center of the well. Little Arnold saw the water rush up, and closed his eyes as the well swallowed him, but opened them to see bubbles sprouting in front of him, bright bubbles, brighter by far than water. He could see two hands, pumping furiously up and down; at his back he felt an irregular thumping, a tugging at his waist—the coconuts another pair of hands yanking him back to the top.

Mottu by the wall watched his son break the surface and flounder around in a circle, the yellow coconuts bobbing at his back. Little Arnold sputtered, but seeing the sheltering wall and friendly faces at hand, he paddled their way, making more noise than progress.

"Over here, Little Arnold," Marie-Santana said. "Come over to this side." She was treading water right next to his father. Mottu and she exchanged glances; she gave him a cool smile. "It's easy," she said to the child. "The coconuts will hold you up. I'll catch you. I'm right here!"

Marie-Santana stretched out her hands to him and smiled, and once again the agitated wavelets rippled out in all directions as he struggled to reach her.

"Move your feet, Little Arnold. Kick! Kick!"

Annabel and Josephine Aunty, watching up above, clapped their hands as he inched forward. Little Arnold looked up at his mother and laughed, forgot to keep up his puppy stroke, and promptly sank beneath the surface. When he came up he found not only Mar'-Santan' Aunty there ready to help him, but also his father, concerned for him and no longer afraid for himself.

Little Arnold felt good. "You'll swim like a turtle, too," Marie-Santana said, back-pedalling till she was again just out of his reach. "Come on, see if you can catch me."

Mottu was unusually preoccupied at dinner that night. His thoughts were on what had happened in the well that morning— he jumping in, Little Arnold on the parapet, and Marie-Santana appearing out of nowhere. Forttu could have taught his son to swim; Forttu was always teaching others how to swim; but no, Marie-Santana had to climb up beside the child and hold his hand and try to get him to jump. Even when the child had refused, and she had jumped in by herself, and he, Mottu, had turned his face half away so she would not think he was there gaping at her, hoping to see whatever there was of her to see, Mar'-Santan' had swum round and round within inches of where he was clinging to the wet stone, and when her face came out of the water for air and her mouth was open, so were her eyes, and she was looking straight at him. Then, when Forttu had tossed Little Arnold in and the boy was dog-paddling as any novice would, she had swum to where he, Mottu, was and called the child to her. Or was she calling *him?* Now he was sure she was. All that jumping in, those fancy strokes, showing off for whom, if not for him? And when she treaded water, bobbing up and down in her tight wet dress, tempting him with her ripe mango breasts—a mating dance, that's what it was. And that smile—how brazen, with his wife standing right there on the parapet. The changeable minx! He should have given her a sign, perhaps a secret sign that he was on to her game and willing, as she was, even with Annabel there at the mouth of the well, peering down at them both.

Mottu had had his share of feni that day, before going into the well and after coming out of it, and also before sitting down to dinner, but now that he was done eating and the vodka-like liquor was a warm glow in his stomach, he leaned over and poured himself some more. He felt masterful; let Annabel object if she dared.

"You've not said a word during dinner," Annabel said to him. She had been watching him throughout the meal and he had as carefully avoided meeting her gaze. "Didn't you like my cooking?"

He seemed not to hear; he had decided to ignore her. Her womanly intuition working at peak level, his wife sent Little Arnold off to do his homework, then came straight to the point.

"If you so much as look at her sideways, I'll kill you," she said.

"Me, look at her?" Mottu said, startled that she had read his thoughts. "Look at whom? At her? Mar'-Santan'?" He laughed hollowly. "She looks at me," he said, drumming his right forefinger on his chest.

He saw at once that she did not believe him.

"In the well," Annabel said. "I'll drown you in the well."

"Can't see how," he said, "since you're afraid of water, and can't swim a stroke."

"That'll make it that much easier," she said.

He puzzled over that, but made no reply. He could not see how it could be done, without her being down in the well with him, something he knew she would never do, and he took a last large swallow of *feni* to clear his mind. But of this he was sure—if she were even half-way serious, she'd find a way.

Later that night, after he had fallen asleep alone in bed because Annabel had busied herself banging pots and pans about in the kitchen, he found he had acquired miraculous powers. With a single arching step he was able to cover as much ground as if he had done the running broad jump; he was gliding through the air in slow motion. Not quite believing what he had just accomplished, he stepped forward lightly again. Starting from the top step of his own front porch, he felt three easy leaps would place him squarely in front of Angelinh' Granny's door. The first took him to within inches of his own garden gate. Landing lightly on his left foot, he bounced off it high enough to clear the gate and land on the other side of the lane. A slight kick off the toes of his right foot and he had cleared Granny's garden wall and was skimming along inches above her steps. Now, standing by the door in Granny's porch, his own home seemed very far away and below him. Nevertheless, he regained his own porch with just one upward leap and a graceful swoop. He felt so good about having done all this that he turned and looked about to see if there were any witnesses.

Marie-Santana was standing in Granny's porch, where he himself had been just seconds earlier; she was looking directly at him and smiling, and as she waved he could see that her dress was wet and tight from swimming and it clung to her figure like onion skin. She put her hand to the side of her mouth so her whispered words would carry more clearly: "Move your feet, Mottu! Come on, move! Quick! Let's see if you can catch me!"

He saw then, as she swayed seductively to and fro, that to reach her he would have to leap over his own well, where Annabel was now standing squarely on the parapet, daring him, arms akimbo.

Steve Davenport

Dear Punch

Frabjous morning, Invader.

Your Judy says Hello Wavy Pattern, Crazy Map. Hello Motel Wallpaper, Heavy Drapes, Pizza Box, Ashtray, Bed. Hello to this postcard. Hey, Stamp. Hi, Wet Spot.

Together we salute you. Hello Bastard. Your Wallop of Yore? Bloat. What rhymes with peek-a-boo.

Callooh from Judy. Callay's mine.

Steve Davenport

True Confessions

1

The ball fields under the old bridge are lit,
the fences are short, and the river stinks
some nights like dead fish and men sweating
after work and cigarettes, beer and piss.
Here the catcher squats, toad in a jersey.
I'm on deck and there's this married woman.

I'm counting the syllables of a line,
thumb to thigh. The guy in the batter's box
jumps away, jerking his bat in short arcs.
He says the catcher's who did it, broke in,

raped his grandmother.

2

Tall chain-link fences criss-cross for back stops.
Long, low fences separate the four fields.
I'm trying to compress things, concentrate,
shorten my swing, elbows in, use my legs,
beat perfect time on my thigh as I wait.
She'll come by later she'll come by later.

I don't know the batter. A dirt-leg friend
of somebody, taking somebody's place.
The catcher's a toad and this guy's a tube
of amphetamines. I'm watching, waiting.

The team is leaning.

3

I'm counting syllables and I'm on deck.
She's married she's married and she's married.
Batter has to kill Catcher with a bat.
I work the midnight shift at the flour mill,
sleep, and drive to the university,
where I read poems about indolence.

I work on a line about a batter
and a catcher, paroled early, who throws
ball one back and nothing happens. I count
the syllables I count the syllables

in motherfucker.

4

Here's what I remember. Men ran bases,
spit, swung bats, swatted at mosquitoes fat
with their blood or after it. I forget
Batter and Catcher, what happened. Married
Woman moved on. Or someone replaced her.
Life anywhere is messy. Here's what counts.

I left the mill for books full-time. I found
poems about work, about compression
that holds me, increases my density.
Every day I write my true confession.

I count syllables.

Renée Ashley

On Infidelity

It has been going on for over a month, in the city, it is not love, it is not even lust, but it felt like the right thing to do at the time, he tells me.

"An affair."

The instant the words are out of his mouth I am emptied. The rush leaves me hollow, deadpan, there is none of the all-too-likely shrieking or catapulting of flatware. Rather, I am suddenly aware that Evan, except for his narrower face and less perfect nose looks almost exactly like Robert Redford.

I cannot get over the likeness.

Nor can I get over the fact that it took me this long to see it. Neither can I believe that this is what I'm actually thinking in the face of what Evan has told me. I know it should be something else. Blaming. Fainting. Throwing. Certainly something else. But I cannot think of what it is I should do.

"... I can't even blame her," he tells me. He looks down at his hands.

I have to ask: "Is it Anne?" I conjure up their faces from the wedding, their guilelessness. I reconstruct the currents of familiarity that shot between them. I feel their champagne under my own nose.

Evan looks at me blankly. He is wholly taken aback. "Anne who?"

So it isn't Anne.

I am relieved. Somehow if it had been Anne, that would have been worse. I am so relieved that I can afford to push it further, take the offensive. I attack.

"Anne who, my ass!"

Then I am condescending: "Schlimhammer, Evan. Who the

hell else would it be?" I talk to him as though he is retarded, as though he needs my help to explain.

Evan is incredulous. His mouth hangs open and, for the first time, those perfect teeth of his nearly drown in the deep pool of his mouth. "Schlimhammer?" His voice starts low and rises, a bird in flight. He understands his position in this conversation all too well, yet he is amused. "Why on earth Anne Schlimhammer?"

I have nothing else to say.

"Who else?" is all I can come up with.

His eyes light on his hands again. He is studying the creases in his knuckles. They fascinate him. "A woman in the pool," he says, meaning the typing pool on the floor above his office.

He does not bother to tell me her name, not how he set it up, where they went, whether she's married. It isn't the point. He feels guilty about her, too.

"I was punishing you, I think," he tells me. He has the eyes of a young boy. He is repentant. "It's silly, isn't it?" He is looking up at me because, so far, I have refused to sit down.

I nod "yes" and think: No, no of course it is not silly.

"What's her name?" I ask.

I think he doesn't hear me.

"What's her name?" I repeat.

He is shaking his head now. His blonde hair falls into his face; he has to swipe at it more than once to keep it from sticking like straws at his eyes. He needs a haircut. Now he is a waif. He has no intention of telling me her name. I know what he is thinking because I know Evan. He is thinking that in punishing me, he has punished her, this unnamed, invisible woman. He is right. It isn't fair, wasn't fair. It stinks.

"Are you going to continue to see her?"

I hear myself say "see her" rather than "sleep with her," "fuck her," "use her." And I am thinking of another, of Hope, and I am thinking that if Evan does not love this phantom woman, or some other woman, that I am lucky, I am in time. I am thinking that this was inevitable. I wished it. I am thinking of all the other things I have wished for, perhaps, and chosen not to see.

Evan looks up. The first sharpness of a growing impatience shrinks his face, wizens it. "I won't see her again. Of course not," he says. He is disgusted.

I finally sit down. I sit across from him, but immediately I see that this is not what he wants at all. When I raise my hand to touch his, he pulls away—I am too hot, too hot to touch, or too sharp, or too dangerous, or, maybe, and more likely, not dangerous enough. He does not want to be understood. He wants to be beaten for his crime.

"Could you have loved her?" I ask him. Not "do you" or "did you," but "could you have?"

"I don't even know her," he tells me. "Not really. It was the chase." He sighs; he shakes his head and I can see that the room and I have melted away for him. He is talking to himself now. "I was lonely," he says. He is confessing. Legitimizing. Qualifying. "I felt wicked," he says. "It was good."

"And it stopped being good?" My question startles him. I am sincere in wanting to know.

Evan does not answer me.

"Does she love you?" I ask. This is a new possibility. I wonder if he has thought about it.

"I don't know." His voice is flat. "I don't think so. I haven't thought about it."

"Well, has she said so? Does she tell you?" It seems such an elementary question now that I have asked it. His pitifulness, and my own impatience, make my bile swell and burst like a boil. "Well, what the hell were you thinking about then?" I shout at him. "What the fuck did you think you were doing? Plumbing the depths of your goddamn soul?"

The outburst sets Evan back only mildly. He has been waiting for it. He watches me, looking for a clue, a giveaway gesture now, but I am a stone wall. He keeps his hands on the table, and when he cannot decipher me, when he sees that I am through yelling but not giving anything else away, he pulls them in closer to his body. "I'm sorry," he says to his hands. "I'm sorry."

I stand. "Me, too," I tell him. I pull down on my sweatshirt, push up at the sleeves, and turn away from him. "Me fucking too."

The room is littered with faces I know I'm supposed to recognize. They are the women she worked with, all who know me by name, who know me in context, with my dead mother laid out at the front of the strange room. They are women who, if they met me on the street, would, without a doubt, keep walking. There are these women, and there is one man, a man who visibly shoulders the weight of some enormous, some debilitating burden which he wears like a shawl across the breadth of his back. I cannot imagine who he is, the husband of one of the women, perhaps, a cripple, or a sick man, or just curious. I cannot recall having ever seen him before. But when he sits amidst the women, distinctly alone, when he bows his head but does not cry, does not speak or pray or look my way, the name comes: it is Herb. He is my mother's lover. His name itself is only a spark, but I am certain of it. I do not know why I know it; my mother would never have told me about him, never anything as personal, nothing so seedy for her daughter to know, a daughter too selfish, too crazy, too distant.

Yet I know his name.

He is a big man, big and broad, with short-clipped gray hair, hair that hugs his big, square skull. He is clean and awkward. His hands, which rest on the back of the bench in front of him, are large and veined, his fingers are tufted with light brown hair like patches of dry weed and I easily imagine those hands moving across the skin of my mother's arms, her back, down her side, and resting at her waist. In my mind, the two of them are dancing, dancing or making love, and they are content. And I am suddenly terribly sorry for the man who is left, this enormous man who carries such a loneliness.

He does not speak to me, nor does he sign the book after he has filed past. His head is bowed, he is invisible, and nearly gone.

It is impossible for me to let him go like that.

I follow him, catch him as he opens the door to an old green Chrysler—and then, for me, a whisper of possibility: have I seen this car before? This man? Are they at all familiar? I touch his arm.

When he turns to me he is frightened, older than I had imagined and frightened. He does not know what I will do or what I may say. He has only my mother's words for how I might act. He looks as though he will erode, crumble, and wash away in the California fog before I can stop him, before I can speak. His own eyes are wide, very wide, bugged from his face in expectation, riddled with red, and as I speak they fill like fountain bowls and spill.

"Herb," I say softly. "Herb, I am so sorry."

It is too much for him, the recognition. His chin falls to his chest and the sound that comes from him seems to emanate from every pore. It is a wail of pain that pours out from the bone, hushed by the flesh. He lowers himself to the edge of the Chrysler's seat, holds on to the wheel for support. He does not look up at me, does not make another sound.

I lay my hand on his shoulder. It looks small there, powerless. Then I turn.

I walk back to the door of the funeral home where women I do not love are gathered, watching me through the glass doors, watching between the stenciled letters and the streams of condensation, and wondering what I am up to.

When I come out again, the Chrysler is gone.

It is not that I have not had lovers. It is that I have not had what I felt were illicit lovers. I am convinced that they must be different, they must be very different. Sweeter? Hotter? Too many people around me are dipping into that particular pot for it not to be different. I wonder what comes first—the seeking or the opportunity? Or perhaps the simple need for a secret? How bored do you have to be? How alone? Myriad combinations, myriad possibilities. Transmutations up the yang, and still I didn't see any of it. It is too much. First I isolate him, drive him to it, then, when he loses his pleasure in it, I beat him over the head with his failure. Yes, I am angry. At Evan. At myself. There is a tumult of jealousy, of responsibility. And no energy left for spite. But I do wonder: who is going to forgive whom in this one?

I just feel so foolish, being surprised.

It is no secret that I pick through reality, pick and sort as though reality were a mixture of beans and stones. No secret that I have treated Evan like a stone.

No, nobody plays it right all the time, and the names, the names are only important when they are all you have.

Evan and I do not eat dinner, nor do we speak much more. We sit on the sofa, both stunned and silent, and we look out the window until, in the dark, we are watching only our own reflections in the glass. It is in that glass that I can see that I am closest to Evan when we are falling apart.

The evening is longer than most when he is home. He brings me tea; I peel oranges and offer him half of each. And when we rise to go to bed, that other woman does not drop away from us as she should, as I want her to; her presence is as strong and as real as the acrid, sweet smell of the oranges, the oil and pulp that has clung to the undersides of my fingernails, to the flesh of my fingers. We are angry and awkward, and at the sound of Evan's bare feet on the wood floor, at the sound of his retching behind the bathroom door, I swear I can see her, though I do not know what she looks like. And I wonder if she loves him, if she has had time to love him, if she is waiting for him now, or if she is using him, too. And I wonder who else has made her feel that way: used, user. And I think that I am naive and that I have asked for this. And that she took me up on it.

I do not know her name, but she does not leave our bed all night.

Greg Herriges

Forgetting John Keats

*Th*wack! The tennis ball shoots diagonally, is struck again, lobs lazily over the net, causing Aaron to hasten to it, presenting him with a timely opportunity to show off his finest tennis choreography, knees bent, broad shoulders pivoting as he backhands the DayGlo orb, sending it in a lazy arc over Julia's head.

I don't play tennis. Instead I watch my girlfriend play tennis with her boss, a man who, next year, is likely to be one of the most important legislators in the state of Illinois.

For just a freeze-frame moment he looks like an imitation of one of his own campaign photographs. The victor. Julia meets him at the net to concede, her smooth arms and legs still May-pale. By July she will be bronze, and when she wears white she will look like a magazine ad for the Cayman Islands, the way she did last summer when we first met at the athletic club. Aaron's hair is cut short, catches the ever-so-slight breeze. His teeth are all even and brilliantly white. When he smiles he could blind you.

"You shouldn't have been able to make that last shot," Julia teases. "It was a technical impossibility."

"I specialize in the impossible," he says.

Julia says, "That's just another way of saying you're lucky, is all."

"*Luck*, my dear, is a word the defeated use to account for the winner's skill." He flashes his campaign grin at me. "What do you say, Tom? Was it luck, or did I have the obvious advantage?"

"I'm afraid I didn't notice," I say, indicating with a tip of my head the twenty or so un-graded essays on the spectator bench beside me. "But I know you've had all kinds of advantages."

Julia tilts her sun visor up and lets her hand rest on my

shoulder.

"Sour grapes," Aaron says. "You're a couple of sour grapes, the two of you. Julia, you'll see to the Greenberger papers this afternoon?"

"I've already called ahead to the office. Stacy's on it right now."

"Good. Make sure she stays on it. I want those delivered by messenger today." And then to me: "So long, *professore*. Learn them kids good."

I have a momentary fantasy of murdering him with his own tennis racquet. I can think of at least three ways to do it.

We lunch at The Grille in Lake Forest. The waitress has brought me an uncommonly well-made Bloody Mary. Two green olives, a black one, a pickle spear, generous portion of vodka. *God bless that girl*, I think.

"You ought to be kinder to Aaron," Julia tells me, from relatively out of the blue. "He picks up on your sarcasm, you know."

"He's that advanced, is he?" She shoots me a look of disapproval across the table, one, I take it, that she has learned from her mother. Her mother was the last one I saw use it, right after we were introduced. "Besides, I thought all he picked up was other guys' girls."

Julia stirs her salad obliviously with her fork. "We're not going over your silly jealousies again. Aaron is the most progressive candidate in the state, and he's going to win the election." Around and around the lettuce spins on her plate, a tiny green galaxy. "And when he does, we're moving to Springfield. What you need to do is stop procrastinating, and start writing your dissertation. Get it over with."

When I first laid eyes on Julia it was something like being electrocuted. In a good way. She was running on a treadmill, and I'd just walked into the gym from the locker room. What first caught me were her eyes, large and bright, and her strength and stature. *Breeding*, I thought, an unusual term to apply to a person, or maybe not. It was almost as though her family's wealth was genetic in nature, monetary ripples just beneath her pecs, part of the package.

Julia is the package, the whole package. And what is one to do when gifted with a package? I've been unwrapping Julia since last August, and I keep looking to see what might be inside.

My straw makes sucking noises. All gone. The ice cubes run aground. I say, "We haven't had the Springfield discussion yet."

"That's because there's nothing to discuss. Aaron wins the election, we move to Springfield, and I run his office. You can always get an adjunct position somewhere, till you get your Ph.D."

I stare over Julia's shoulder, through the front window. A man gets into a silver-gray Maserati, backs into traffic, and zooms away. Just like that. I wonder how someone gets to that point in life. You could buy a condo for the money.

I don't tell Julia that the problem with progressive politicians is that they are still politicians. I don't tell her that I've already made an appointment for tomorrow with Dr. Sommerdale, my dissertation advisor. I don't tell Julia a lot of things.

The click of my heels upon the scuffed linoleum floor echoes off the painted cinderblock walls. Here and there fliers taped at chance angles advertise club meetings, tutoring at discount prices, student concerts. One reads *Dare to Live Today*, a lecture series. Down the dimly lit hall a young woman practices musical scales discordantly on a violin, and I want to tell her that I am too old for this, for any of this, thirty-one on my next birthday, and that really she ought to stop that awful screeching, right now, please.

When at last I am sitting before Dr. Sommerdale, I can't take my eyes from a small piece of netting that has escaped like a tiny traitor from beneath the widow's peak of his hairpiece. His office is closet-small and there is not a smidgen of breeze, of anything that remotely resembles ventilation.

"Mr. O'Connell—" He prefaces every sentence with my surname. "—your dedication to the subject of Keats and your knowledge of his letters are admirable indeed, but this notion that you can determine what his mature world view and philosophy might have been, had he lived, is . . .well, problematic, to say the least. I'd nearly rather suffer another lurid study on his relationship with that Brawne woman, though it's been done to death. Everyone these days is Keats-crazy. I still haven't forgiven him for 'Endymion.' What a lot of sheer rubbish *that* was. He should have been horsewhipped!"

"Dr. Sommerdale, he was dying of consumption."

"Well, don't look at me that way, my boy. *I* didn't give it to him!" And with this he leans back in his chair, closes his eyes, and is lost in a euphoria of unpent cackles and chortles for fully a minute or more. When at last he comes out of it, his cheeks reddened, his forefinger wiping stray tears from the corners of his sagging old eyes, he suggests, out of breath, "Mr. O'Connell, now, really, Byron is greatly superior to your cockney friend. Wouldn't you rather do a bell-ringer of a dissertation on him?"

The netting. I am tempted to reach my fingers to his forehead and tuck it under the old moth-eaten toupee. Either that or rip it off his head and go running down the hall, scare the violinist with it.

When I tell him no, he brings both his hands down in fists upon his desk blotter, as though he might beat me till I change my topic proposal. Then in one movement he picks up a fountain pen, uncaps it with his thumb, and begins writing furiously something in large, florid script. If he had produced a quill, an inkpot, and a bottle of laudanum, it would not have surprised me. Upon completion, he slides the paper across his desk to me. It reads: *The Dark Age of John Keats.*

I say, "What's this?"

"That is the new title of your dissertation."

"But what does it mean?"

"You are going to chronicle, in scholarly detail, the manner in which John Keats was forgotten during an entire generation, before he was rediscovered, and before all those later editions and adaptations of that damnable poem, the one with Porphyro hiding in the closet, what's it called—"

"'The Eve of St. Agnes'."

"Precisely. Now off with you. It's time for research."

It's time for beer, I think, more to the point. I drive my navy blue Geo Metro to Lake Forest's The Lantern, and begin my tour of world beers. I am soon in Belgium, drinking a Stella Artois, and looking forward to The Netherlands, and a pint of Brand. By the time I make it to Germany, I know (after grading another essay on "How to Build Your Own Computer") that I do not want to beg for my choice of study.

I am discovering myself though negation. I do not want to go to Springfield. I do not want Aaron even vaguely associated with my life. Somewhat stunned, I realize that I am growing indifferent toward Julia—beautiful, strong, well-bred Julia. What in God's name *do* I want? Perhaps the answer is in Prague. Not in Prague *per se*, but in a Czechoslovakian beer.

No, it isn't there. I leave my car on the street and walk home; I might not know what I want, but I know I am past my limit, in danger of having my drinking passport revoked.

· · ·

This morning I am in the university library, eating chocolate bars (a tobacco substitute) and reading all I can find about Keats's death and the days to come. It will probably take me years if I go through with this—the letters of his circle, Charles Brown, his beloved Fanny Brawne ("*That Brawne woman,*" as Dr. Sommerdale referred to her), Joseph Severn. Ah—Severn. Severn the painter, the faithful friend, kind and caring to the end. Keats practically coughed himself to pieces in Severn's arms—Severn had not a thought for his own welfare, for the very real danger that he may himself contract consumption. All those days and nights locked up in their little place in the Piazza di Spagna, Keats half in love with death because he knew he could never grow to be the poet that he was certain that he might have been. I need to know what he was thinking, what he wanted to write now that he could write no more.

I slam shut the volume that I have been reading. One hour till my 101 section, and still four or five papers to go. I brush through one called "Making a Killing on eBay," and another, "Changing Your Car's Oil Is an Art Form." I jot notes about tense consistency, the use of objective case pronouns. I unwrap a Hershey's Milk Chocolate bar and devour it in one, two bites.

Then there is an essay called "Hina Matsuri and The Japanese Day of Re-birth." The student—Akemi Morioka. I am transported to Japan during the month of March. Spring comes early, "delicately upon the sensibilities of young girls, ardent to share their Hina-ningyo with family and visitors alike." A set of fifteen dolls in ancient ceremonial costumes is laid out upon the steps of a little house. An emperor, some musicians, ladies, ministers—there is an empress, also. As Akemi puts it, "The emperor has a grave air of dignity in contrast to the fragile, light days of the new and fresh season. Springtime make my heart feel as though tiny sparrow birds dance within it."

The vaulted ceiling of the library has not crashed down upon me, and that fact alone comes as a shock, for what are architectural principles compared to the explosion of words that I have just read on this plain, white page. How do the joints stay fixed in place, secured, in the presence of such simple, honest beauty? What are they against the elegance of Akemi's "Hina Matsuri"?

• • •

I met a lady in the meads,
Full beautiful - a faery's child,
Her hair was long, her foot was light,
And her eyes were wild.

It is the summer session of English 101, section 007, a rhetoric class. We have spent two weeks on modes of writing—narrative, process, and extended definition. Without any warning, I give a seminar on British romantic poetry, focusing on Keats's ballad, "La Belle Dame sans Merci." Four or five confused students give me the shady looks I have coming. Most of the others couldn't care less if I were talking about transitions or past participles. What I try very hard not to do is take in the details of Akemi Morioka's face, which are finely sculpted, animated, as though she can barely contain her enthusiasm for life, a spiritual radiance which is natural, but nearly blinding. All this I skim from the corners of my eyes. I wonder how I could have failed to notice her before.

Have I mentioned that I quit smoking? I quit twice last month and once this week.

"Mr. O'Connell," an impatient objection from a tall youth with a ponytail. He sits in the corner and grimaces at me, most of the time. He has clearly had enough.

"Yes—Jason, is it?"

"Jordan."

"Of course, Jordan."

"I don't want to sound rude or anything, but what's all this poetic stuff got to do with extended definition?"

An unsettling rustle of voices follows. I recognize it as the prelude to a mutiny.

I say, "Jordan, you like baseball, don't you?"

He shuffles his feet, which are ensconced in big, brown lace-up boots beneath his desk. "Well, yeah."

"Think of it like that, then. Curve ball. Change of pace."

After class I sit alone in the adjunct office, reading a letter from Keats to Fanny Brawne, date uncertain, perhaps July 15, 1819. It is an embarrassing series of confessions, and he complains that she is disinterested in him, but he tries to make it sound as though he is not carping, rather carrying a kind of cross of the heart. There are times (like this) that I could grab the ailing Keats by the collar, shake him, perhaps even slap him across his face—lightly, just to get his attention. *"Do not let her do this to you!"* I want to say.

There is a knock upon the open door, a slight rapping, three times. I look up, and it is Akemi.

"Professor?" she says. I shoot to my feet, dropping the volume closed.

"Akemi," I say. "Come in, come in." There is no chair for her, so I slide one out from the desk next to mine, wheel it just before her, extend my hand in a manner of invitation.

"I hope I am not troubling you," she says.

No, no trouble, I assure her. There is that flashing about her again, an effulgence, and I discover that it comes from her eyes. She is a slender woman of about, what—twenty-nine, thirty, perhaps?—although there is a timeless beauty about the features of her face. And she wants to know if she is troubling me.

She sits, then flicks through the pages of her notebook till she finds what she is looking for—the handout of "La Belle Dame sans Merci," the poem that I presented in class. She places it upon my desk, and very deliberately, with great purpose, she traces the lines of a stanza with her delicate forefinger, and searches my face with her eyes to see if I comprehend her concern, the import that lies there.

> I saw pale kings and princes too,
>   Pale warriors, death - pale were they all;
> Who cry'd- 'La Belle Dame sans Me
>   Hath thee in thrall!'

I nod a few times, uncertain, and she nods with me, as if that will help me understand.

"I see, Akemi. But what is it?"

Her mouth purses in a momentary "o" shape. Then: "She has stolen his *heart*."

And so I will have to start smoking again tonight, this afternoon, as soon as possible.

"Yes, she has. That's very good, Akemi. That is exactly what she has done."

That appears to be all there is to it. She nods once more, gravely this time, and places the poem back in her folder, as if returning a valuable document to its place. She stands. I stand.

She begins to leave, but then turns suddenly, her eyes enunciating a question before her lips can catch up. "She is not a *bad* woman?" She asks this as if she wants assurance.

"No," I say, "she is not bad. She is mysterious, and she is very beautiful, perhaps of a different world."

And then—and this is completely unexpected—she bows to me. Out of reflex, and a great deal of appreciation and awe, I bow back. Two, three times we perform this gesture, and then she is gone. Just the silence of the room punctuates her absence. There is half a package of cigarettes in my briefcase.

"You have to start taking this seriously, Tom. Think of it as a business merger."

I have stopped by The Deer Path Inn, an old, stately hotel and restaurant, for one drink with Julia, and to cancel our plans for this evening—all those English 101 papers. We were supposed to see a concert. She is not pleased.

I sip my wine. I slip a Three Musketeers bar from the breast pocket of my sport coat. "Let me see if I get this straight. Getting married is like a business merger?"

"In every way. Two entities joined together, getting tax breaks, compounding capital, sharing assets, a common goal."

"You romantic, you. Sounds like Aaron's version of love."

She stirs the ice cubes of her cocktail irritably, avoiding my eyes. "Aaron leads an entire county. He makes plans and gets things done. All I know is, you and I need to settle our future, and only one of us is trying."

Settle the future. I wonder how it is that you go about getting the future to concede to your terms, to turn out exactly the way you want it to.

I say, "Buy a Prius? Build a McMansion in the suburbs?"

Julia bristles. "What's wrong with an environmentally friendly car, and a home in a safe place?"

I am half a world away as I ask, "Did you ever have dolls as a child?"

She folds her napkin, places it squarely upon the table, lifting her purse from the floor. The evening is over. "I'm talking about our lives, and you're eating candy and talking about toys. I make plans, and you break them. And when do you suppose we'll get another opportunity to see James Taylor at Ravinia?"

With any luck, we won't.

· · ·

In Rome, lying in his little room, feverish, despondent, Keats refused to open the letters from Fanny. He would see the shape and color of the wax seal, know it was hers, and look away. Had her flirtations, her apathy so destroyed him? Or was it like his writing itself—which he had also come to neglect . . . a love that had no future because *he* had no future? Had he finally floundered upon something that even his great imagination could not transcend or bridge?

I read right on the floor between the stacks up on the second floor of the library, reclining my spine against the shelves till it aches. Poor Keats—sallow, perspiring through his English cotton shirt, the coarse wool of his only suit. Mother gone. Brother gone. A thousand miles interceding between himself and his beloved. His dream of being a great poet—an eternity away. But which mattered most—his lost love, or his ruined art?

Today I have prepared a lesson on "Lamia" for my confused and unsuspecting students. Lamia, Keats's strange female vampire-serpent, disguised as a beautiful woman. She enchants and seduces. She could probably manage state political campaigns. But after I carefully set my text upon the podium and look out at the class, there is an immediate and conspicuous absence, one that, for me, at least, might as well be a rip in the fabric of the time-space continuum.

No Akemi.

And so I give an improvisational lesson on extended definitions of abstract concepts—loneliness, for instance. Emptiness. Confusion. Class runs short and I return to the shabby shelter of the adjunct office. Beside me is a worn copy of *The Oxford English Dictionary*, one that has been duct-taped along its spine. The only other presence in the office is old, retired Dr. Reemers, who plays chess against a computer software program for hours at a time. Strategic intellectual masturbation. *How does someone end up like that?* I wonder.

It is nothing, a chance discovery, as I mechanically check my email: an ad for instant hair re-growth, another urging me to sell my precious metal, some pornography that got past the university spam catcher. And just beneath that—"From your student, Akemi Morioka." I click it open at once.

Dear Mr. O'Connell, Sir,

This is your student, Akemi Morioka, with news I wish not may disappoint you. It sadden to say I had to return to my family's home in Tokyo to care for my ailing auntie. I will email my definition paper to you, if you find the practice acceptable. Perhaps I return to the United States sometime, but for now I must remain. I hope my letter finds you in good health, and that you approve of my essay. I use the Japanese-English dictionary unsparingly.

I will always treasure memories of your class, and your helpful direction.

Yours,
Akemi Morioka

I read it twice. Then again, this time taking apart each sentence, reading each word with the inflection Akemi would have given it, hearing the gentle music of her voice. Soon I feel as though "little sparrow birds dance in my heart," to quote a remarkable but relatively obscure poet.

In the far corner of the office Dr. Reemers has just checkmated himself.

My apartment is tiny—a two-floor walk-up in Lake Forest, Illinois. Across the train tracks outside my window is the house in which Genevra King grew up, the girl who spurned F. Scott Fitzgerald and by doing so shot him to lofty literary heights, telling him that rich girls do not marry poor boys. It is for sale, the house. It can be yours for six million dollars. A steal.

I am surrounded by books—books on the floor, the coffee table, the tiny kitchenette counters. Keats, Keats, and more Keats. I read on the floor, curled up on a worn rug. Paisley pattern. Looks like it has thrown up upon itself. Once Fanny got word of Keats's death, she shut herself off in some kind of self-imposed house seclusion for about two weeks, and then never mentioned him again, except in rare instances. Word got around in poetic circles that Keats had been smitten by some mysterious *femme fatale*—inspired at first, and then struck dead of a broken heart. The truth was something else again. Fanny was a mousy little thing of no distinguishing grace or beauty who enjoyed minor league coquetry at military balls. While Keats, increasingly subscribing to a Platonic concept of artist-as-receptacle-of–the-divine, literally bled to attain poetic immortality, Fanny wanted to boogie.

But she had kept Keats's love letters.

I light a cigarette. All out of chocolate. I can always quit again tomorrow.

Fanny is partially redeemed—until I open another volume and discover that she instructed her son to sell the letters after her death. They would get a good price on the market. Keats had no offspring to benefit financially from the expressions of his great love and desire. The beneficiary was a subsidiary of an entirely different merger.

Of course now, one must take into account Fanny's young age. She was just a girl, and genius can be a burden. What did she know of the pangs that send an artist (even if that artist sees himself as nothing more than the agent of divinity) on a quest for beauty? And for how long could Keats have kept up that intense level of passion?

I think of Julia, see her in the future in a green suburb, in a newly built house with the obligatory bourgeois turret. I look for myself in this mental picture and wonder where I may be—perhaps in the den, penning a brilliant analysis of "Hyperion," or else sold off into indentured servitude to sustain the weight of the mortgage.

There is another book I have borrowed from the library, *Leave Your Shoes at the Door: How to Avoid Culture Shock in Japan*. It is my new constant companion, worth its weight in yen, which, I learn, is pronounced *en*. Should a funeral car pass you, you must hide your thumbs. And how about this—in Japan you do not take a bath to get clean. You sponge bathe yourself and rinse and then get in the bathtub—to *soak*. The number four is considered bad luck; it is pronounced like the word for death.

A-ke-mi Mor-i-o-ka. It is not so much a name as a melody.

$$\cdots$$

"Tom? Do you know what time it is?"

I am standing at Julia's apartment door, which she keeps half-closed behind her, her naked foot propped against it. I am not entirely sure why I have come here, though I think it has something to do with the rising sun and travel.

"Tom?"

"It's two in the morning," I say.

From inside, Aaron calls her name languidly, with just the slightest hint of a question at the end. We stare at one another. Julia's face slowly droops from the expectant cover-up freeze. "I didn't mean for this to happen," she says to me.

I do not know what to think of this development, whether I should walk away in a huff, go inside and use it as a good excuse to murder the bastard, or congratulate her. There will be no merger after all. A friendly takeover has transpired. The commerce of love.

"What the hell," I say. "A girl's got to dance, right?"

Her foot moves slightly and the door closes. She folds her arms across her chest, narrows her eyes. "What is that supposed to mean?"

"Nothing," I say. "It's just something I read."

I am halfway down the hallway stairs when I hear her call, "But what will you *do*?"

She means without her, I realize. Julia cannot fathom anyone's world without her. But I can. At last, I can.

Outside the dark morning air is cool. I walk alone down a sidewalk, the world unconscious behind closed doors. Well, most of the world. I discover a spare Almond Joy in the pocket of my windbreaker. If it weren't only done in musicals, I might click my heels.

. . .

You mustn't do anything rash, I tell myself, as I book one-way passage to Tokyo on the Far East Airlines Internet web site. It is a very good price, and so I compliment myself on keeping my head. I am wonderfully calm. Wonderfully, ecstatically, wildly calm. Next, I write a note to the Dean, explaining that a family emergency has come up—which is true. It's Akemi's family, but he does not need to know that.

The landlord—oh, hang the landlord. He can keep my furniture in lieu of the six months rent I owe on the lease. It's worth less than half of that, but let him try to find me in Tokyo.

I wonder how long Julia has been sleeping with Aaron, surprised at a sudden ember of jealousy. *No matter*, I tell myself. *Don't go down that road now, of all times.*

And so, dear Akemi, unexpected business brings me to your city. I do hope that you will be able to find time to perhaps be my guide as I learn my way around Kotoku, near your auntie's home, discovering the fine points of your rich culture.

Your presence in my class and in my heart will always be a golden treasure.

Yours,
Tom O'Connell

I hit the *send* button, aware that I have just altered the trajectory of my life's orbit forever—an astronaut of love. How magnificent the world looks from up here—all mine again.

The Artistic World View of the Mature Poet, John Keats

Dr. Sommerdale fingers the document hesitantly, as if someone had just placed a fresh turd before him. His eyes, overly moist and swollen with age, look up from the paper to me.

"Tell me what it is that I'm looking at, Mr. O'Connell."

"The title of my dissertation," I say, "which, by the way, my entire oversight committee has approved, with the exception of you, that is."

"You got Dandler and Wycroft to sign off on this?"

"Yes, sir."

He mumbles something indistinct, nods to himself, and pushes the paper a good way across the scarred grain of his old mahogany desk.

"My boy," he says, almost apologetically, straining as if to help get the heft of his meaning across, "it's just that I don't see how you can establish what *would* have been if it never *was*."

Today his toupee is a touch off kilter, the netting once again fully exposed. He starts slightly as I reach out and tuck the fabric beneath the hairline, and pat it in place.

"Why, Dr. Sommerdale, with all due respect—sometimes the only way we *can* know what might have been is if it never was."

Like that mental picture of Julia's future house, for instance, the one with the phony turret and all that green lawn, I think to myself. *No wonder I was never able to find myself in it.*

I consider for a moment that I do not deserve this happiness. But yes, I do. Certainly I do. It's amazing how many socks with holes I have in my dresser. Out they go. I would be laughed out of Japan in those things, my brogues parked at the front door. And now with the full committee's approval, I will keep Keats alive. Gasping and hacking, but alive in the hearts and minds of readers forever. *Sayonara, English 101 students. Goodbye, old Dr.*

Sommerdale. Balls to you, Aaron. Ohayoo gozaimasu, Tokyo!

I lay down a final item in the scarce room of one of my bags, a Hina-ningyo doll I have purchased, a gift for Akemi. It is an empress in a red wedding kimono, elegant, her face stoic beneath a striking silver hat, white as a kabuki player. *My dearest lady,* I rehearse as a salutation, for when I appear at her aunt's door, shoes in hand. It is a greeting that Keats sometimes used in his letters to Fanny. Or is that too formal? *My dearest Girl*, another of Keats's. That's it. The tenor is so important, the fine points of personal communication precise in their intent. The kimono is a subtle detail, I think, though unmistakable. In any case I can always claim I did not know it was ceremonial wedding garb.

On my lap top I save as a favorite site an English library page I will use while I write my dissertation in the mornings, over tea, no doubt. In the afternoons, the Japanese air faintly scented with blossoms, Akemi and I will take long walks, and I will learn of her childhood, her dreams of the future, her desires, though I believe those are hardly hidden or arcane.

A tone sounds from the computer. I have new email. The click of the mouse, solitary, final. *Akemi!* I think, and my heart rises to my throat, until all too soon, it falls.

Mr. O'Connell, Sir—

As much as I truly would like to honor your request to serve as your guide in my city, I am sorry to tell I will be unable. My husband's United States visa have expired and may not be renewed at this time. He come to join me in caring for my auntie, and I must also assist him to find suitable position in his field of engineering.

Fervently I wish that your time in Tokyo is pleasant, and that you obtain a guide suitable to your needs. Have safety in your travels.

Fondly,
Akemi

I stare at the computer, my gaze abstracting, until the Times New Roman letters become nothing more than dancing random black shapes upon the screen, the room lit by its white glare. After several moments I see that there is an addendum at the end of the note, just the tops of the words visible, petals on the surface of a pond, until I scroll down.

P.S. Professor—perhaps the faery child lady did not intend to steal the heart of the knight at arms. Perhaps it were accident.

Dan Turèll

Deep Frost Film

(translated from the Danish by Thomas E. Kennedy)

And then you say to me
in a low confidential tone
and with a sudden direct slightly nervous gaze
directly at me on the sofa
that there's something you would like to talk to me about
and when you say that I know what it is
because otherwise you would just say it, right?
and I know it has been boiling up all afternoon
and your steps have said it and your walk has whispered about it
and you have held your cup in a way that says it, too
so it's no surprise
but now it comes
and I look over at you
and past you, not to stop you
and look out the window at the neighbor house's unmoving rooftop
with a sprinkling of snow on an icicle beneath the window ledge
and as if by an invisible action the music goes lower
                                        on the phonograph
and becomes very still and melancholy
and from somewhere the light dampens
suddenly I see a spot on my tee shirt
and everything stops and hangs in the air
even the dust motes don't care to lie on the carpet—

And that's when you say it
in that quiet tone you use for divorce and deaths

and I know every word of it
and you know that of course also
and while you say them because you feel you must say them
and of course you must
I look out the window to the neighbor house's unmoving rooftop
who knows if something similar is happening
under the sprinkle of snow and that yellow light
who knows what is happening to them
in that little room over the icicle
this late afternoon—

And that's when you say it
and I almost can't think while
my head runs away from me
it drives blocks forward at full speed
it concentrates on the neighbor's icicles
icicles everywhere in the world
all life's icicles in all phases of melting
it glides into the music from the phonograph that now grows
louder again
and further over the bedspread I smoothed a couple of hours ago
and the dishes that have been washed
except for the usual forgotten cup in the living room
my head gathers purposeless old telephone numbers together
it calculates the sum of the digits of your birthdate
it sees you that afternoon when we met
and that weekend just after when we—

And then you've said it
and the record is over
and I know it all very well
and I still don't look at you

but at the neighbor's motionless rooftop
and take the single forgotten cup out to the kitchen and wash it
before I go—

Elisabeth Murawski

That's Life

He's with a much younger woman
on the Yellow Line train.
I'm sitting right behind him,

his graying buzz cut, a white
athletic sweat band hugging his head.
It's the Lou Rawls ache in his voice

that floors. I quit reading my book,
the poem about changing the names
of paint colors: "Nerves"

for the frost of stars. Imagine
waking up to those vocal chords!
I wonder if he talks, a bee

making honey, cruising the cape,
the hip of his Lady Love. When
they exit at L'Enfant Plaza,

I get a better look. He's stocky,
paunchy, moves as if, dancing,
he'd float like balsa wood.

She takes his arm. They disappear
into the swarm of tourists. Len
comes to mind, classical piano

major who called me "precious,"
charmed away my resistance.
That voice. The caramel skin. His

hair would be grizzled now, too.
Ours was a muddled ending,
a telegram full of STOPs.

Elisabeth Murawski

The English Teacher's Wife

It's one of those art cards
you write your own message in.
A young girl in blue,

the oval face and long neck
unmistakably
Modigliani. Inside,

one line to him:
All is forgiven.
Unsigned, anonymous

as the poem
he's always loved
to the western wind.

I slump in a vinyl chair,
the card alive
with questions.

I look at my drugged
husband, priest
to all my secrets,

restless, tossing
in his bed,
in too much pain

to see or care
I am tearing up
"The Servant Girl."

Elisabeth Murawski

Maytime

Jealous of the blonde you dated
that spring, she of the lisp
and wasp waist, I was glad to hear

you would not be hers but God's.
As we walked in Grant Park, everything
that night was moonlit, reverent:

the clouds speeding overhead,
the eloquent jets of Buckingham Fountain
cheering your sacrifice in fits

and bursts of varicolored lights.
We Poles can be idolatrous, adore
a Roman collar. I felt privileged

to know you. Should I have waited?
My marriage, like your calling, died
young. I met her once, your wife,

the ex-nun. She asked me not to smoke
in your house. Each Christmas you wrote,
always late, when the tree came down.

Once you sent a photograph. What
were you thinking? To show how gracefully
you'd aged? I kept it in my wallet

for years. Had I been in a wreck, cops
would have thought you were my husband.
That's not why I tore it up. Hope

has to fly. As I dropped the pieces
from my hand, I felt light, transparent
as a Mayfly's wing. Something broke.

Susan Tekulve

Cherokee

Sadie plaited the last of her mother-in-law's hair, winding the long, white braid around the back of Emma's head, pinning it in place with a rhinestone clip. She sifted through the dresses in the wardrobe, choosing a white tea gown. Emma sat still while Sadie pulled the dress over her head and fastened the tiny hooks all the way up the back. Sliding the wheels beneath Emma's rocker, Sadie rolled her to the window to look out over the wild roses that Sadie's husband, Dean, was planting for his mother on the high, sunny ridge beside the house. It was early spring. The whole hillside flamed with orange azaleas and yellow daffodils, and the old pond stream that Dean had rebuilt gurgled cleanly, fiddlehead ferns tucked between its stones. Emma would not look out at the garden. She stared into her lap, gazing inward, a piece of white paper clasped like a handkerchief in her knotted, ladylike fists.

"What have you got there, Mother?" Sadie asked.

Emma's fingers tightened around the paper, and Sadie guessed it must be one of the love letters Emma's husband, Caleb, wrote to her on his lunch breaks at the Norfolk and Western station in Bluefield thirty years ago, before he was shot down by a tramp beside the tracks. The shock of his death had quickened her rheumatism, hardening her spine, legs and feet, until she never stood or walked again. She spoke very little now, spent most of her time reading the love letters she kept locked in the heart pine chest in her bedroom, beneath the oil painting of a sad-eyed Jesus sitting on a high and rocky precipice at midnight, overlooking Gethsemane.

"Is that one of them old love letters?" Sadie teased.

Sadie knelt beside her mother-in-law's rocker, and the old woman's fingers unclenched, releasing the note into Sadie's hands.

The paper felt warm, soft as flannel from all the unfolding and folding. *I saw Dean kill that little girl,* Sadie read. *Go tell him to turn himself in.*

"Mother, where did you get this?" Sadie asked.

Emma stared through her empty hands into her lap, her eyes filled with long distance. The woodstove sighed. Sadie thought of tossing the note into the flames, but its words had rekindled a question in her mind. *What little girl?*

Sadie folded the note, slipped on her worn flats and cardigan. She stepped out onto the front porch, looked down the gravel drive, toward the blue cedar guesthouse where Dean had been spending most of his time since his last heart attack.

The spring before, a week after he was released from the hospital, he'd driven to Cherokee to walk the medicinal trails and learn the healing properties of wild herbs. He'd come home late the next day, spilling a bag of coins across the foot of the bed, showing Sadie the buffalo nickels, Mercury dimes, and trade silver dollars dating back to 1885. He said he'd gone into the Dollar General and seen the cashier giving a young woman trouble about trying to buy food with her dead grandfather's coin collection. He started pulling out his money and bought all the coins from her.

"She was just a little girl," he'd said. "I thought I was helping her. I didn't know what I would find." He'd put the coins back in the pouch, slipped the pouch beneath the folded handkerchiefs in his top dresser drawer. Then he mentioned that he'd brought the girl home to live in the guesthouse, that maybe she could help Sadie out with his mother while their daughter, Hannah, was at school. He closed the dresser drawer and shook his head. "You have to wonder what happens to people like her that don't get help," he said. "Hard times."

The Cherokee girl never helped out with Dean's mother. She stayed inside the guesthouse all day long with the curtains shut, smoking cigarettes and eating the butter lettuce, tomatoes and snap beans Dean had picked from Sadie's garden. He worked on the guesthouse every day, claiming its shower kept backing up.

When her commode overflowed, he brought in a backhoe and began digging up the leech bed, cleaning out the septic tank. He became so distracted with fixing the girl's plumbing that he began neglecting his own house and garden. The wild roses mildewed. Fallen leaves clogged the bottom drains of the pond stream. The goldfish overpopulated themselves, caught bacterial infections and turned belly up in the basin.

In late August, after she'd scooped the last dead fish from the pond stream, Sadie went looking for Dean. As she knocked on the guesthouse door, the lace curtains mingled with a figure wearing a white dress Sadie recognized as one of Emma's trousseau gowns, sewn by an immigrant aunt, impossibly elegant for farm life. Emma had kept them all in the pine chest with the old love letters from her late husband. As the girl backed slowly into a pair of shadowy arms, Sadie backed away from the house, not wanting to see whose arms were holding her in the darkness. Her heart chilled and fisted as she walked back up the hill. Her whole body filled with a frozen wakefulness, she stayed up all night waiting for Dean to come home, sitting straight-backed on the bench beside the piano, unplayed since Emma began failing. She was still waiting for Dean at dawn. When he finally came walking out of the woods and into the house, Sadie could not bring herself to ask if he'd been in the guesthouse with the girl. She knew the answer to that. She couldn't bear to hear him say it. Instead, she asked about the dress.

"It suited her," Dean had said. "I thought someone should get some use out of it."

"Your family is your charity," Sadie said, crossing her arms across her chest to end the argument.

Dean had taken the girl back to Cherokee, but he'd never apologized, and they never spoke of the girl he'd kept for a whole spring and summer in the guesthouse. He stayed outside, hauling rocks down from a secret place at the top of East River Mountain, repairing the old pond stream, planting more fiddlehead fern between the stones. He slept alone in the guesthouse. The next spring, Sadie went out into the woods and dug up a wild rose bush to give him, a peace offering he could plant beside his pond stream. Dean stopped when he saw her, his face falling softly with disappointment.

"Oh, it's you," he'd said, already turning his back to her, heading inside the guesthouse. "I thought you were—"

Her, she thought, dropping the rose bush, running back up the hill. After that, Sadie stayed inside the big house, careful not to cross him on any path, nursing her mother-in-law's body until she felt more dull and spectral than this tiny, bird-like woman he'd brought to live with them now that she no longer could live alone in the big house up on Wilderness Road. Sadie began dressing Emma every morning in a different trousseau gown, as if to justify her demand to get rid of the Cherokee girl. The women of this family get plenty of use out of those dresses, Sadie thought, each time she buttoned or hooked her mother-in-law into one of the dresses. She bathed and dressed and coiffed Dean's mother every day, as if repeating a charm that might bring her husband back to her one day, though it never did.

Dean was inside of the guesthouse now, Sadie was sure of it, but she could not go down there. She couldn't bear another falling look of disappointment in his eyes, his turned back, his shoulders stiffened by the sound of her voice. Sadie dipped her hands into the pockets of her cardigan, fingering the sharp corners of Emma's strangely cruel note, feeling the mixed urge to punish and defend him. She began to question her husband's random act of devotion to a stranger. What if that girl really was only a charity case? She had to wonder what had happened to her since she'd been sent away. Sadie had wanted her gone, not killed. Surely her husband, who took such pleasure coaxing plants into life, gathering and stacking stones into a beautiful stream, did not have it in his nature to murder anyone, especially a young woman in hard times. As she thought of the unfortunate girl, Sadie's chest ached, and a chill dread settled over her skin, sinking slowly into her veins, draining her arms and legs of all strength. The only way to fight this leaden feeling was to flee this house that had never felt like her own, the woods that hedged and silenced it.

She went into the bedroom and ran her hand across the bed, her husband's side neatly made up, her side unmade. She tried to recall when he'd stopped wanting her, when he'd first turned away. Had this happened before or after his illness? She called her mother, Jane, who'd gone gaming in Cherokee with her first husband, Sadie's father. Sadie asked Jane if she remembered the way to Cherokee.

"You planning on doing some gambling on the reservation?" Jane asked.

Sadie pictured her mother standing beside the single barber chair in the beauty shop she'd been running from her cabin on Dump Hill since Sadie's father left.

"Do you remember the way you took to get there?" Sadie asked.

"Well, if Bluefield, Virginia, is the gates of hell, you go three levels down, and turn west," Jane said.

"Mom."

"Oh, girl," Jane said. "That was so long ago. I can't remember my own name sometimes. How do you expect me to figure all this out?"

"I just thought you might remember something from before--"

"Why do you want to go all the way back there?"

Sadie knew better than to confide her marriage troubles to her mother. Sadie's father had left the year her older sister, Grace, died of stomach cancer. Jane had married three more times, but none of the other marriages took. When Sadie was seventeen, unmarried and pregnant by Dean, Jane urged her to get rid of the unborn child, warning her against marrying a man whose mother was still alive and in charge. Sadie went through with it all, the pregnancy and the marriage. It was the bravest thing she'd ever done, marrying against her mother's wishes, her one rebellion against her outlaw mother.

Waiting out Jane's silence on the other end of the line, Sadie's heart banged inside her ribcage, and her throat fluttered. How easy it would be for Jane to point out that she'd been right about Dean, that Sadie's twenty-year marriage had been a risk taken, and lost. Sadie braced herself for Jane's long-awaited chastening, feeling vaguely that she deserved it.

"You still take the old road, number 441," Jane said, quietly. "I don't know what you hope to find when you get there, but that road can get lonely in the level places."

After hanging up the phone, Sadie went over to Emma's room and shifted through the wardrobe where she'd hung the trousseau gowns. In a playful moment, she'd named each one, calling the nightgown "A Gap in the Hedge," the going-away dress Emma wore after her wedding "I Missed the Boat Upon Which I Should Have Sailed." She put on the going-away dress. The tea-length skirt crumbled as she hooked the waist, and a few of the pearl buttons popped off the blouse as she fastened them. She walked over to the vanity mirror.

She hadn't thought of her own body for a long time. She'd lost weight from the physical labor of nursing her mother-in-law, and for the first time in her life she had cheekbones. Tired of fooling with her hair, she'd cut it all off, and it curled around her face in an old fashioned bob, making her eyes look large and startled in her pale, thin face. She'd never been a great beauty, but the big eyes and high cheekbones might have made her look younger under different circumstances. Standing in the beautiful antique dress, she appeared faded, used-up. She backed away from the mirror, walking through room after still room of the house, many of them closed off, bedsheets covering the heavy furniture. Dean had painted the house that spring, forgetting to prop the windows open so that they wouldn't stick. This is marriage, Sadie thought. A silent house full of unused rooms whose windows were all painted shut.

She wandered back into her bedroom and opened Dean's dresser, found the bag of coins he'd bought off the Cherokee girl. The pouch was a child's suede marble bag, dyed purple, stamped with a yellow caricature of an Indian wearing a tall headdress like those worn by the Western prairie tribes. Dean had told Sadie that he'd dropped the girl off at her father's house on the reservation, that she was waitressing at one of the tourist restaurants. Though Sadie had never gone anywhere beyond these mountains, she suddenly wanted to get away, go anywhere, be anonymous in a tourist town. She placed the coins in her other dress pocket, the one that did not hold Emma's note. She weighed out what had been taken, and what must be returned.

Sadie went outside and looked at Dean's Model B Ford parked beside the house, the key always in the ignition. It had belonged to Dean's father, and Dean still washed and waxed it every week, calling it his "moonshine coupe." Climbing behind the steering wheel, she hoped the car would make it to the Smokies.

I'll take my chances, she thought as she turned over the engine. She bounced the car down the rutted gravel drive and onto the paved road that wound beneath East River Mountain until she reached the tunnel. On the other side, the high land unfolded, smoothing into rolling pastures dotted by solitary black barns. Chestnut horses walked slowly along the split rail fences, grazing around still farm equipment bowing in the center of pastures starting to green in late-May sun.

As Jane had predicted, the road's level places were lonesome. Dean's cigarette scent rose up from the car's upholstery, bitter but familiar. Sadie considered turning the car around, heading back through the mountain, telling Dean that she was having one of her migraines and had gone to the pharmacy for her headache powders. Maybe he'd take her down to the guesthouse and lay her across the brass bed, rub lavender oil into her temples, as he'd once done to ease her headaches. She longed to feel his rough, frostbitten fingers on her face, even if that touch felt like charity.

But the time to turn around had passed. As she crossed the North Carolina border and neared Asheville, the Smokies looked dark blue, distant, the paler ridges swelling behind them like memories of mountains. She drove until the rain hit the windshield, two big drops, then a blinding cascade. Sadie closed her window. The hard rain sealed and silenced the car, and the tobacco began to smell stale, illicit, one of her own family's secrets. Her mother had been a nurse during the war and had kept the uniform. Sometimes, after Sadie's father left, Jane put on her nurse's dress, claiming she liked the way she could still turn a man's head in that dress. She unbraided her hair so that it would sway softly at her waist as she walked downtown and into the nearest bar, where she would drink and play cards with the train men, sometimes bringing home one of the men who'd lost to her in a game of stud poker. Sadie often heard them fumbling in the next room, but the men were always gone by morning, as if they never existed.

Fog rolled over the mountains and across the road, softening the panic that had sent her speeding away from her house. The downpour dredged up a new and different doubt. What would Dean say when she got back? Would he be angry? Worse yet, would he even notice she'd been gone? She thought about turning around, but all the road signs—Maggie Valley, Tribal Bingo, Ghost Town—urged her forward. On the exit road for Cherokee, she bypassed the entrance for the casino, turned left at the brick reservation school, its windows finger-painted with yellow flowers and a blue river. To the right on main street, a strip of weather-beaten motels called Newfound Lodge and The River's Edge flanked the Oconaluftee River, their cedar balconies jutting out over the cascades.

Beside the last motel on the strip, a young and an old man danced on a tented stage in front of a diner with a light-up sign out front boasting, "Authentic Native American Cooking."

Sadie pulled into the parking lot and walked over to sit behind an elderly couple on a wooden bench. The younger man wore a cut-off tank shirt and a high prairie headdress made of bright red and white feathers. An eagle tattoo was burned into his bare, muscular arm. The older man was thin, short, and wiry, his still-black hair cropped close to his head. He stood at the back of the stage, his arms crossed, wearing deer skin leggings and a delicate, beaded vest. Sadie thought he looked more authentic than the drummer, more dignified, his slate eyes looking beyond the dwindling crowd of off-season tourists.

"I'm Lone Wolf, and this here is Chief Graybeard," the drummer said into a microphone. "He's going to show you the warrior dance."

The older man crouched, stepping with the slow drumbeat, shaking a gourd rattle over imaginary prey. He stalked across the stage, turning toward the audience, staring in mock menace. When the music ended, he ducked into a teepee guarded by a mangy, stuffed buffalo.

"And now Chief Graybeard will show you the most difficult dance," Lone Wolf said. "It's called the hoop dance. His great grandfather taught it to him when he was a boy. He's the only one left who remembers the steps."

Graybeard came out of the teepee, carrying five plastic hula-hoops that he set out on the stage in a row. The hula-hoops disappointed Sadie more than the drummer's prairie headdress. She looked back at the sign in front of the restaurant, feeling unaccountably betrayed by the sign's promise to be authentic. She stood to go, but the drummer looked right at her.

"Of course, Graybeard and his great grandfather would have gone down to the river for willow branches and made them into hoops. But the Chief draws his energy from a source even more mystical than the willows."

Sadie sat again, wondering, What could be more mystical than a willow? The rain came down harder, but she could hear the river's rush above it, the drumbeat pounding beneath. Graybeard picked up each hoop, stringing it along his arm like a giant bracelet. He turned slowly, moving the hoops over his body, until the circles formed an eagle's wings spanning his shoulders. He crouched, forming a turtle shell across his back. He continued spinning and moving the hoops across his body, the drumbeat pounding in Sadie's stomach, frightening, thrilling, until she forgot all about the hula-hoops being plastic, and she imagined Graybeard dancing down by the unseen river, beside willow limbs that arched and swirled like long hair across the water, their cut wisps bending easily with his body as he shape shifted into a hummingbird, a butterfly, a spider's web.

When the music stopped, the dancer bowed to the crowd and went back into the teepee. The drummer spoke into the microphone.

"Let's give a hand for Chief Graybeard, the hardest working guy in America, the most photographed man in North Carolina besides the Reverend Billy Graham."

Graybeard came back out of the teepee and passed around a woven basket. "The Chief just got out of the county correctional facility," the drummer said. "He and his family would appreciate your tens or twenties."

In her rush to leave that morning, Sadie had left her purse at home. She reached into her sweater pocket and felt Emma's note. She considered putting it into the basket, dashing back to her car, driving back home. She reached into her other pocket, found the coin pouch and dropped two of the trade silver dollars in the basket. The chief nodded, "Thank you, pretty lady." She blushed, relieved by how he'd accepted the coins as gracefully as if they were a ten or twenty. She ran back to her car.

It was dark now, sprinkling, the wet air so black she no longer could see the mountain looming across the street. The long drive through the rain had made her sleepy. She considered renting a room in one of the motels, sleeping until the sun rose and she felt rested enough to drive home, but she had only the coins left in her pocket. The roadside chief had accepted those coins. Maybe someone in the restaurant would take a silver dollar for a cup of coffee.

Inside the diner, the walls were bright blue, adorned with dream catchers and wooden masks. Cactuses in southwestern-themed pots lined the windowsill above the cash register. Sadie sat at the counter, and a waitress walked over.

"What can I get you, Sweetie?"

"Will you take these coins for a coffee?"

The waitress nodded. "The money police don't live here anymore. You can pay with what you've got."

Sadie ordered a cup of coffee with cream, a basket of fry bread.

The waitress brought the coffee, and Sadie wrapped her cold hands around the warm cup, studying the three waitresses to see if one of them could be the owner of the coins. One girl filled salt shakers, the second wiped down tables and the third dried water glasses. Any of these girls could have been the one Dean had brought home with him, but none looked as if she'd ever been a runaway or a charity case. Their black hair tied back, they moved like sure-footed dancers, their dark eyes pleasantly absorbed in closing tasks. Sadie felt a soft pang of loneliness for her daughter, for her lost sister, for the company of any woman who hadn't grown too old for a conversation free of grief and bitterness.

When the waitress brought the basket of fry bread, a man slid onto the stool beside her. He offered his hand. She recognized him as the older man who'd performed the hoop dance. "The name's Graybeard."

Sadie shook his hand. "I'm Sadie. I saw your dancing."

"Sadie, Sadie, pretty lady." Graybeard said. He lifted up a jar of honey, poured it over her fry bread. "If you're going to eat that, you may as well eat it right."

Sadie unwrapped her fork from its napkin, took a bite. The warm honey burst across her tongue, spilling out one side of her mouth. She ate quickly, swabbing the plate with the last bite of bread. The man handed her the napkin. Sadie put down her fork and dabbed at the corners of her mouth as daintily as she could.

"I must have been hungry," she said.

Graybeard laughed. "It's all right. I liked watching you eat."

He took out a pipe with a bowl carved like a bird, its stem strung with two tiny feathers. He tamped down the bowl, lit it. Sadie breathed in the smoke, recalling her mother smoking wild, sweet tobacco in a dainty pipe at her kitchen table.

"My mother is part Cherokee," Sadie said. "She used to smoke a pipe like that."

"I thought we were from the same tribe."

"What do you put in your pipe?"

Graybeard smiled, nodded toward the cactus plants lining the windowsill. "Some of my relatives go out West every summer to live with the Old Settlers. When they come back, they bring stuff with them."

He signaled the waitress, and she brought a kettle of hot water, a clean blue cup.

"Here, try some of this." He poured hot water into the cup, sprinkling green buds from an unlabeled tin can. The buds unfurled, darkening the water. Graybeard stirred sugar and honey into it. She sipped, wincing from the bitterness beneath all the sweeteners.

"You didn't like my dancing, did you?"

Sadie took out the coin pouch. "All I had on me are these coins—"

"I don't want to talk about your money. Tell me why you didn't like my dancing."

"I liked your dancing." Sadie paused. "I just didn't like your hula hoops. They weren't ... authentic."

Graybeard looked down at the Indian head on the bag of coins, but he continued to speak in his rough, good-natured voice. "My family has been here since the white settlers thought up Manifest Destiny and kicked most of us out of these hills. My great grandfather hid in the cliffs above Deep Creek and fought the government during the Removal so that we could stay. My family signed the civilization treaties, but we never promised to be authentic," he said. "If you want authentic, go to the museum down the street."

"I'm sorry," Sadie said, pouring more sugar and honey into the tea, trying it again, wincing at the bitterness that no amount of honey could disguise.

"Don't be. I come from a long line of people who never did anything they didn't want to do. Besides, kids love seeing an Indian. I'll bet you always wanted to be Pocahontas when you were a little girl."

Sadie smiled. As a girl, she'd wanted to be anyone but Sadie May Musick, the good daughter of a lawless woman who styled hair for railroad wives who praised her clever hands and high cheekbones, but never befriended her. On days the train men came for haircuts, Jane sent Sadie outside, telling her not to come back until it was dark. She'd spent long hours roaming the woods and rivers, pretending to be an Indian princess.

The tea eased her shyness. She began enjoying Graybeard's company. After so many months of her husband's silence, she liked this man's easy-going conversation. She tried to keep him talking.

"You ever want to be somebody else?" she asked.

"I used to be a policeman," he said. "I started chiefing by accident. A gift shop owner asked me to fill in when the regular roadside chief didn't show. This was before the casino moved in, and I made more money that weekend from chiefing than I did on the police force in a month. I kept doing it because I could take care of my family no matter what the government did," he said. "I've always found ways to get around the federal government."

"If you've always gotten around the government, why were you in prison?"

"I lost this restaurant in a poker game to Lone Wolf on my forty-fifth birthday. I tried to stake my wife to get it back. She got mad about that and divorced me. Then she had me put in jail for failure to pay child support," Graybeard nodded toward the waitresses. "Those are my daughters. Lone Wolf lets them work here to pay off some of my other debts. He's got a little room in back where he lets me sleep."

"That's terrible," Sadie said.

"What's terrible? Another man would have taken my wife."

"Well," Sadie said. "I don't think it was very nice of him to take advantage of your ... sickness."

"Gambling isn't a sickness," he said. "It's more like a resurrection. Every time you lose, you die. Every time you win, you get to be reborn." Sadie frowned, still unconvinced. "Let me explain it a different way," he said. "Around here, B.C. means 'Before Casino.' Before the Casino, all Indians were just a number. If we married outside the nation, our children became one half an

Indian. If they married their children became one fourth.   We had to carry cards to prove we were a fraction of ourselves.   If we got caught carrying an Eagle feather, we were fined $10,000.   Now, with our earnings from the casino, the tribe could *buy* an American eagle.   We're still sovereign over the Qualla Boundary.   That's one hundred square miles of land.   We're building a new school and a hospital with the casino money.   We're sending all our children and grandchildren to college."

He took out a leather pouch, loosened the drawstring and poured two dried butter beans across the counter. The beans were painted blue on one side, white on the other.

"Here, let me teach you a traditional Cherokee game."

"Is it older than your hula hoop dance?"

"It's as old as these hills," he said. "Each person takes a turn flipping a bean. The light sides are worth six points. The dark sides are worth four. The first person to reach twenty-four points wins."

Graybeard scooped up the beans, side-arming them across the counter.   When both beans landed dark side up, he slapped his hand on the counter. "Eight points."

Sadie took a turn, rolling out one light and one dark bean. "Ten points," she said.

He took his time now, and she grew impatient, eager for him to tip his hand open and cast the beans so that she could take her turn.   She rolled two blue, and he rolled two light.   The tea had eased her worries, blurring the memories of Dean's retreat into the guesthouse, softening the words in his mother's note.   Sadie felt the thrill of losing, the giddy hope of winning something back.

"Twenty-four," Graybeard announced, sweeping the beans back into the pouch.

He picked up his pipe, tamped down the bowl and lit it, watching her face.

"So what have you won from me?" Sadie whispered.

Graybeard leaned closer. "A kiss."

"Right here?"

"Meet me in the back."

She laughed, but he stood abruptly and headed toward the back of the restaurant. Sadie sat at the counter, feeling too old for a stranger's kiss, especially one that might take place in the back room of a diner on an Indian reservation, possibly over a reeking toilet. Her mind felt cloudy, unfurled by the mysterious tea, still capable of asking the most obvious questions: *Why didn't a man called Graybeard have a beard? What kind of husband stakes his wife in a poker game?* She wanted to run back to her car, lock the door and sleep beside the river until it was light enough to drive home. She left some coins on the counter for the fry bread and coffee. The pouch felt lighter as she walked to the back of the restaurant.

Graybeard's room was made of rough-hewn wood, furnished with a single cot pushed up against the far wall, a framed print of a Cherokee rose hanging above it. Near the back, a glass patio door opened out onto a balcony that overlooked the river. Sadie stepped onto the balcony and stood beside Graybeard. The moon reflected and split like two sides of the same white coin on the water's black surface. The cool air and river water cleared her senses a bit, but the tea had begun working on her like a truth serum. She thought of wheeling Emma down to the Catholic church in Bluefield once a week so that she could make a confession. Sadie had always wondered what kind of sins could have been committed by a woman who'd sat silent in a house for thirty years after her husband died. Now, she understood her mother-in-law's urge to confess without sin or shame, her need for someone who would listen, unsurprised by anything she could tell. Sadie took the coin pouch out of her pocket and showed Graybeard the buffalo nickels, the bust half dimes, the trade silver dollars.

"My husband came here last spring," she said. "He bought these off a Cherokee girl who was having a hard time. He didn't know they were worth anything until he got them home." Graybeard looked down at the phony Indian head on the pouch, his face unreadable. "He brought the girl home too and kept her out in our guesthouse." She told him about her husband's obsession with the guesthouse plumbing, her own untended garden, how she made

Dean send the girl away. She stopped, pulling her mother-in-law's note from her pocket. "His mother gave this to me this morning," she said. "It made me worry about what happened to that girl. I came up here to find her, to make sure she was all right and give her back the coins. I suppose it was a foolish notion."

Graybeard took the note. He read it, letting the frail paper flutter over the water, and for a moment Sadie hoped he might release it into the wind, let it tumble down the river, let it sink into one of the dark, trout-filled places.

"Maybe this note bothers you because it's partly true," he said.

Sadie waited to hear which part was true. Above her, the moon was as bright as it had been on the nights Dean courted her, when he'd taken her out riding on his quarter horse in the woods at night. At the time, he'd seemed so much older than eighteen, a grown man walking ahead on the trails, expertly naming the wild herbs in the undergrowth—mint, wild ginger, watercress. She'd believed everything he told her back then. Now, she understood that she'd been just a little girl, taken in.

Graybeard folded the note and gave it back to Sadie.

"What should I do with it?" Sadie asked.

"If it was me, I'd take it out into the woods and bury it," Graybeard said, moving toward her. "Now. Come over here and let me fix your plumbing."

His kiss was soft, but not tender. He tasted of smoke and honey and the bitter tea they'd both been drinking. She started as his sharp tongue twisted slowly against her own. He kept his eyes open. When she looked into them, they were flinty and dead.

She pulled away from him. "It's getting light out here."

He shrugged. "I like the light, you like the dark." He led her into the room, sat her on the cot and knelt before her.

"When I saw you standing in that white dress in the rain, I thought you were a vision," he said. "I nearly had a heart attack."

Sadie's heart flipped as she recalled Dean's weak heart, those first twilight days of mourning his lost health, how he'd turned away from her in his grief and how, eventually, she'd turned away from him. Her husband hadn't murdered anyone, but his shadow life in the guesthouse was killing. She flushed, her skin itching inside her mother-in-law's ill-fitting dress. Whatever had possessed her to wear it?

Graybeard put a cool hand on her face. "You're burning up."

"It's this dress," she said. "I can hardly breathe in it."

"Take it off."

She paused, deciding. "I will if you don't look at me."

He pulled the blanket off the bed, making a pallet on the floor. He lay down and closed his eyes. As she began unbuttoning the dress, he laughed, "If you had the courage to cut your losses and leave your husband, I'd fight to win you. I'd keep you here with me."

She stopped unbuttoning herself and looked up.

"I don't want to be fought for," she said. "I don't need to be won or kept. I've been feeling ... dispossessed lately, but I don't think I should be here. I think I should be talking to a preacher, or a priest."

Graybeard leaned forward. "I can be your priest."

He reached for her, but she put a hand firmly on his chest. "I don't think that would help either of us."

"Can you do one thing for me before you go?"

She nodded, and as he started to unbutton her blouse, her hand flew up to block his hand.

"I promise," he said, gently stilling her hand with his own. "You need this."

She dropped her hand. As the dress fell around her waist, she felt free of its weight. He ran his finger along her collarbone. "This is pretty," he said. He cupped her face in his palm. "Good bone structure." He continued touching and naming the pleasing features that most people overlooked when they saw her. He unhooked her bra and held his face against her chest. His head soft against her skin reminded Sadie of her daughter at age two, when Hannah liked to press her head against Sadie's chest, continually amazed by the discovery of her mother's heartbeat. Sadie closed her eyes and heard him murmur, *I'll bet myself against yourself. I'll bet my feet against your feet. I'll bet my legs against your legs.* His smoky voice sent a wave of heat through her, fevering her whole body. She desired him. She broke out sweating, thick rivulets of water pouring between her breasts, pooling at her waist. The river rushed outside the open back door, loud as a waterfall, its noise filling the room. She closed her eyes, feeling pleasantly soaked, relieved. It had been a long time since she'd wanted anyone, but she did not move beyond this strange embrace. It was enough to simply want again.

When he let go of her, Sadie buttoned her dress and stood. At the door, she looked back one last time. Lying back on the pallet again, Graybeard had set the two silver dollars she'd given him upon his eyes. Already, he was cutting his losses, fading. She had the idea that if she stayed with him, in this dim room, she'd disappear too. Sadie held the coin pouch in her pocket. Judas coins, she thought. Already, with the silver missing, the pouch felt lighter.

"You still want to know what I put in my pipe?" Graybeard asked.

"Yes."

"It's the breath of gods," he said. "Maybe tomorrow, maybe next week, I'll rise up and live again. We're going to have an uprising."

Outside the restaurant, she sat in her car before the stone overlook, beside a sign that read "Swim at Your Own Risk." The moon's reflection had disappeared from the river. Watching the brown water run high beneath the white sky, Sadie allowed herself to hope for her own uprising. She imagined her husband kneeling above the pond stream behind their house, planting another wild rose she'd bring to him, his head bent, as if he were atoning. She could see herself burning his mother's note, offering the ashes to him with the morning's tea leaves, telling him it was all compost. As the two stood side by side, trellising the vines along the garden wall, he'd offer back, "If this rose gets its legs, it should stand on its own and bloom again in a year, maybe two."

On the other side of the river, ravens bounced on the branches of spruce growing from the muddy bank, preening their shiny black wings. She started driving. Ahead, clouds draped around the dark mountain like torn and faded batting.

R.A. Rycraft

Keeping Tabs

On Valentine's Day seven years ago—the year my youngest turned sixteen—I set-up my Facebook account. This was the year I would figure out social networking, or so I thought. I wasn't getting any younger—I turned forty-five February 13—and felt a pressing need to keep up with my kids.

Valentine's Day was never my favorite holiday. Why did it matter so much? Perhaps because it made me think about marriage, or think about the mediocre marriage I was finding increasingly lopsided.

I got the Facebook idea from Sheila at church. It's a fact, Sheila claimed, that you're able to keep tabs on the family without anyone feeling spied on, and that was exactly what I was aiming for. I thought the kids would be happy Mom was on Facebook. I wanted to be their friend, and I assumed they'd want to be mine. It occurred to me that I existed in a sort of hourglass, slipping through the lives of my children like trickling sand, and that these five precious young adults would welcome more contact with me, even though I dimly suspected the reverse was probably true.

I had an idea of how Facebook was supposed to work. There'd be the kids, of course, and I'd be able to check on their status to see what they were up to and look at their pictures and see who their friends were, but I'd also find people I'd lost touch with from school or past jobs or old love affairs. Sheila guided me through the more complicated aspects of Facebook, which were many, given I was technologically impaired. I stared at the computer screen for hours trying to figure out what to include on my information page, ending up with:

Favorite Quotes: There is no such thing as conversation. It

is an illusion. There are intersecting monologues, that is all.

—Rebecca West

Interests: Camping, Motorcycles, Gardening especially, Keeping up with my kids

Basic Information: I am joyful in all that I do.

Relationship status: Married 26 very long years

I searched my way to fifteen Facebook friend requests, including Sheila and my five children, among others. Sheila's page was intimidating. There were videos of her kids' soccer games, dance recitals, birthday parties, first Holy Communions. There were several photo albums filled with dozens of pictures.

My kids' pages weren't so elaborate. They were filled with comments like,

Why can't I sleeeeeeep?!?!?

I had a dream last night that I was getting drunk on Pabst and Bitch's Brew while playing Halo and yelling at random siblings. It was fun.

I'm worried that one day you are going to wake up, look at me, and scream because you don't remember who I am.

Alone on Valentine's Day? Not me.

The ability to peek into their lives made me uncomfortable—of being unseen, undetected, potentially witnessing, maybe for the first time, who they were outside the rules, protection, and boundaries of our home. Also, I hadn't counted on Facebook's hypnotic allure. I was quickly hooked, which became a problem. But on that day, what did it matter? The weather was bad. My husband, Matt, and I weren't going anywhere. In fact, he'd left a phone message saying he'd be home late. Valentine's Day was *not* our day. He had grown beyond it; I could live without it. Now that the day was just like any other day, I couldn't remember why I'd cared so much about it years ago.

Instead of planning a romantic dinner, I spent my time surfing Facebook walls, which I could do without being "Accepted" as a friend because, back then, most people didn't set their privacy to "Friends Only," including my kids. The only thing I couldn't do was post notes: *You are not permitted to perform this action.* Otherwise, there were many lives open for anyone to examine. Like Leah, my kid, twenty-one at the time, who posted pictures of herself with two girlfriends: Leah bent at the waist, resting her forehead on one girl's stomach, leering at the camera, in her hand a live bong, the other girl pressing herself against Leah's behind, holding her waist. *Charming.* My kid must have left her head on the upper shelf in her closet among the battered stuffed animals and Collector's Edition Barbie dolls when she decided to post those pictures. I wasn't ready for such images. The slutty effect was *unnerving* to say the least.

It wasn't long before I had nine friends so I could actually "talk" on some walls, or what appeared to be talking, without getting into too much detail. I thought my comments were private and seen only by the person whose wall I was visiting. I didn't pay attention to the Newsfeed; otherwise, I might have gotten a clue sooner about who might see what, words whipping onto who knew how many computer screens with their intended and unintended meanings. At the same time it seemed benignly attentive, as if someone was interested in what I was doing and rewarding me with a happy smiley face.

On a whim I looked up Matt. To my surprise, my reclusive and anti-social husband had a Facebook page. He'd had it for more than two years. His site was more detailed than expected—in fact, it was more revealing than Sheila's, which seemed funny . . . then. It didn't seem to me that he had time to mess with Facebook— there were eleven projects he was assigned at work, according to him. Although he wasn't in the habit of bringing work home, he spent most evenings alone in his study with the door closed, the tapping sound of a keyboard filtering through. Now I guess I knew what he was up to in there.

But good housewives ignore hints of their husbands' mid-life crises, right? Why borrow trouble? This too shall pass. They can't help it. Studies show men go through a sort of menopause, too. Matt seemed no exception. He'd posted a profile picture I'd never seen, a nice picture of himself, standing beside what looked like the trunk of a giant tree on some white sandy beach in some tropical paradise, wearing tight blue jeans, a white button-up shirt with sleeves rolled, a wide-brim suede hat, sunglasses dangling from his ring-less left hand.

In actuality, we hadn't been to any tropical paradise since the honeymoon we spent in Hawaii. With five kids in tow, all we could afford were the desert, the Colorado River, or Lake Mead camping trips we planned in the vain hope that spending time together outdoors—riding quads and motorcycles and wave runners and waterskiing behind borrowed speed boats—would translate into quality time as a family. That all of these trips were fiascos accounted for Matt's decision to build a swimming pool in the backyard. Once decided, no further camping trips were planned. But the minor detail often ignored during the retelling of the no-more-trips story, by the kids and by Matt, is that the pool was never built. The perfect father the kids frequently describe was the paternal image the kids preferred to that of a father who didn't keep his promises.

My husband looked quite the buff dude in his profile picture. He'd grown more and more obsessed with diet and exercise in the past few years—his potbelly shrinking, his arm and leg muscles growing hard and defined, his butt toned and firm. Funny that I didn't view him as good-looking. But then the man who came home to us most nights bore little resemblance to the man in that Facebook profile picture. That Matt seemed relaxed and he was smiling and the smile reached his eyes and he looked happy. He seemed to be embracing . . . something . . . new people, new experiences—life. He stood beside that tree, struck a pose, said "Cheese," then probably retrieved the camera and continued his walk along the beach alone. Alone was a state he found preferable. Whenever work sent him on business trips, he always went alone. He insisted that all of us stay home. Despite their ages, he was particularly insistent about not leaving the kids to fend for themselves or leaving the house unsupervised.

So the picture was probably taken on one of those business

trips, a trip near some strange seashore. Strange to me, that is. I was mesmerized by the image. What I didn't get was why he'd never mentioned his presence on Facebook—why the secrecy when it was perfectly reasonable to have an account for business, networking, and keeping in touch? And the secrecy went deeper than Matt hiding his Facebook account from me. I discovered all five kids—Leah, Orie, Veda, Edie, and Ray—among his 213 friends. How long does it take to acquire 213 friends, anyway, and who are they, I wondered, because I certainly didn't recognize many of their names. And then there was his relationship status: NA. NA? What was that supposed to mean? Not Available? Not Applicable? Was he married, or wasn't he? And even if he meant Not Available, why not just write it? Why not just write "Married"?

I felt like I was watching my life shrink, except all the important pieces were still there. My husband was still mine; my kids were still home. I was Me the wife, Me the mom, becoming Me the bystander. That fateful Valentine's Day it was late when I got to his page. I didn't intend to read many of the posts on his wall, which was fine because I wasn't there to spy. Well, maybe a tiny bit. No, I told myself, I just want to look around quick-like, see what kinds of things he has to say. He was quite chatty, actually. Often, he recommended links to songs, YouTube videos, and *Daily Show* clips with a *Check this out* comment. One of his friends seemed to "Like" just about everything he posted—a twenty-something, red-haired fairy princess, firm where I'd gone soft, face serene and absent the tense fatigue present in the face I look at in the mirror. Ena Story was her name. She wore a bright, form-fitting, flowery dress, far removed from the comfortable black and white outfits I dressed in. She was dolled up and posed like a Paris Hilton wannabe: laid out on a patch of green grass, eyes closed, one hand combing her fan of red hair while the other rested on her breast, joint ashes poised to tumble onto her chest. Lips curved in a slight smile.

Which made me think of my wedding dress—a puffy sleeved organza gown with a full skirt and Chantilly-lace overlay, a Bo-Peep-ish style typical of the 1980s. Why had I given it to the girls? Why had I let go of something most women treasure, as if foreshadowing my future life—my life as an old woman alone? Because it meant nothing. I was cleaning my closet, came across the dress, and thought *I'll never fit in it again.* Poof! Out of my sight. Into the toybox. I suppose I shouldn't have done that. Bad omen. Or a symbol. The subconscious already checking-out, getting rid of the wedding dress followed by the wedding cards. Anniversary cards. Ancient Valentine's Day cards. I couldn't remember the last time he gave me any kind of card, or the last time he wrote the words, let alone said the words, *I love you.*

You know when it's over? When the anniversary and Valentine's Day cards you've saved for twenty-six years go into the same trash bag as the clumped kitty litter.

I read through all of Matt's posts. I noticed that week after week, and then day after day, my husband and Ena Story engaged in decorous Facebook chats in which people at work were funny, families were regularly crazy-making, and life was an evolving diet plan. They worked together at White Brandt & Co. And there were pastimes in common: learning to fly airplanes (something he'd talked about since day one but never done anything about), running marathons (Ena Story having recently run one at Diamond Head), motorcycle riding, hiking at Irvine Regional Park. Causes like "Protect Baby Seals" and "Relay for Life" littered their posts. All the odder, then, that Facebook seemed the place to meet, to talk about their shared interests, instead of some restaurant or motel.

Buried in Matt's Newsfeed (along with Ena's *I want a cupcake . . . or two,* and some guy's *Women, why do they weep?*) was Leah's *I've led a far riskier and more disreputable life than my mother.* Was she bragging? Was she proud? Where did she get such immodesty? Leah, who are you? And Matt, who are you?

On his not-so-private wall, the Ena Story posts kept popping onto the screen: each one phrased with careful, innocuous precision. A status update: *I may be in a slightly better mood today – the jury's still out.* And Ena Story replying, *Do you need a do-over?* Matt wrote, *Yes, I do, thank you very much.* Ena Story wrote back suggesting, *You could take a break and eat a muffin.* Then some guy named Richard Roth wrote, *LOL.* Somebody else just posted a laughing smiley face. After that, the thread stopped, ending without a period.

I discovered a *Race for the Cure* team photo, everyone wearing black wife-beater T-shirts with the slogan "White Brandt's Booby Team" splashed across their chests in turquoise letters—the *W* hot pink and tweaked with a ribbon effect. And in the center of the picture? Ena Story, wearing hot pink short shorts (butt cheeks probably hanging out the backside), pink Converse high-tops, and a thick black headband holding back all that red hair. A feathery turquoise boa hung from her neck, and her arms were draped across the shoulders of the men on either side of her—some guy I didn't know and Matt—his head leaning against hers. The caption read: *Susan G. Komen Race for the Cure at Fashion Island in Newport Beach. What an amazing event and what amazing people. Great work Booby Team!* The image was suspiciously benign, as if a public display of affection suggested there was nothing to hide.

"Why can't we join your team?" I had asked Matt before the race. I still took some interest in him: he was, after all, *my* husband, though I'd been negligent, I realized. Regarding myself critically I saw: *the woman had let herself go.* Stomach flabby, butt bulbous, the arms too flaccid, the hair too fried. There was no make-up on the saggy round face. I should have done better.

The day I asked to go with him on the *Race for the Cure,* he had gazed at me with exasperation. "The team is for employees," he said.

"That doesn't make sense," I told him. "Why would a fundraising team turn away people—six additional people from this family alone—willing to help raise funds?"

Matt looked at me. "We are a running team," he said.

This was absurd. I tried not to raise my voice; my husband always clammed up when I raised my voice. "Running team?" I said. "There can't be any walkers?"

"You're raising your voice," said my husband.

"I am not," I said.

"Because it's not going to do any good," he said.

"What's not?"

"Keeping at me until you, until you . . ."

"Until I what?" I said.

"Get your way," he replied. "You're not going! You can't run with us!" By this time his face had turned a deep shade of red. He gave me an indignant stare and thrust his finger in my face. "You should see someone about that OCD," he told me.

"I know," I said. "You're right. I should see someone." Then I had to go into the bathroom and lock the door, because my eyes burned and I never let Matt see me cry.

There was a post dated December 31st that hit me like a sledge hammer. *Better to have loved and lost than to live with a psycho for the rest of your life.* And Leah writing: *I love it!!!!!*

He shouldn't have done that. Portray his wife as a psycho, or psycho as wife. It was too much for me to sort out. The willfully oblivious have trouble with concrete evidence, and perhaps I had more trouble than most.

Anyway, I should have known better than to write my suspicions on Facebook. I told Sheila about Matt and Ena and his so-called work trips to tropical islands, and how I fretted about women our age hitting menopause.

Sheila responded: *Do you ever read peoples' posts on here and think to yourself . . . You, my friend, are quite odd, and I never knew until I started reading your posts. You are still my good friend who thinks everyone is an idiot. Haha. Love you. Next time, message me.* ;-)

And I wrote: *Please don't pay attention to me. I'm diminished today. Terminal. Out of sorts and likely to stay that way.* :-(

Flower Conroy

God Trace

Eve pressed her gun
to your shoulder.
A white-whiskered dragon clawed
up from her thin jeans, sinking
its milky talons into her ribcage.
Her machine stirred
below your surface,

its hum conjured: a crushed hive
or a boot's breaking of a book's binding.
You struck a match, lit a Lucky
Strike, inhaled smoke as if breathing in the dust
of an angel then offered
it to her. She took it between her patent leather lips

& continued stitching flesh tapestry with fluid thread.
Buds of dew blossomed, blood pooled
from the emerging tattoo. With a rag she smeared red
across your arched back's sun-starved skin.
With her mouth she smeared red
across your famished mouth.

I could no longer watch through the basement
window. I relinquished—your image embedded
in my mind, a stain. I crossed
the streets, sought the sanctuary of my car.
Eve forward & backwards, branding
your back, Eve crying
out, her dragon dancing.

The car engine vibrated against the cold.
I drove without destination,
passed a billboard that promised:
Jesus Saves. I marveled
how the difference between a cross & a
crucifix was a man. How the difference

between sacrifice & sacrilege
could be dissolved into suffixation.
And ultimately, how one difference
may make all the difference. Like if it were one
degree colder there'd be the possibility tonight
for indifferent snow.

Flower Conroy

Astronaut Affair

Circus in the sky. You left before
I could read the clouds aloud
to you; now this fusion.

The sun slinks into the cold gown
that is November's midmornings.

I think of your train of cages
to the moon—not to the moon,
but to moon's ... what is it?
Open outer space embrace,
where you embark, pioneer
of cosmic sideshows.

I walk out onto the balcony
to smoke. The edge of weather
gnaws my fingers.
Who loves a spaceman?

A thousand light-years you dance
across sky, stratosphere, ozone.

On another planet your ultrafamily
smiles when you walk in the door.
Your doppelgänger dog squeaks &
exposes its plutonium belly.

You put down your suitcase;

take off your helmet.

Honey; honey; honey.
Your home is my alone.

Flower Conroy

Decapitation

I
cut your
face out of all
the photos.
Not to

ex-
scind you
but in attempt
to see your ab-
sence. To see
what I look
like

from
the outside without.
I peeped through each hole
to absorb what your vacancy gazed.
The walls were the walls, the television,
the television. Unchanged in its flux, the
lava lamp was the same fuchsia lava
lamp. At my feet, scissors amidst
the confetti of decollated
heads, all yours,
staring up at
me.

Dennis F. Bormann

Fish Hawk

Whom do we love? I thought I knew the truth;
Of grief I died, but no one knew my death.

—Theodore Roethke, *The Sequel*

He watched the osprey soar on the thermals. With a dip, its wings pulled tight into its body, the bird plunged toward the St. Johns River. As it reached the surface of the water it pulled up from the dive, deftly plucking a fish with its talons. The bird lifted its prey into the air with slow, powerful beatings of its wings, and headed towards the mangroves. Its aerie is probably there, he thought.

"David, did you see that?

"Yes."

"Gorgeous bird." Her eyes were wide with wonder.

"Poor fish."

She turned to him and stared. Then laughed. Her eyes returned to the brilliant flash of sunset the osprey disappeared into. The last light of the day played in her hair. Auburn. Red and golden highlights. Splaying over her shoulders onto her back.

"That's one thing you have to say about Florida."

"What?"

"The sunset."

"Right." He turned away from her and watched the river. A large fish struck the surface with a loud slap. He saw the concentric wave widen, then disappear quickly in the current. "Jennie," he started, "I don't know how to say this except straight out." He felt her attention and he swallowed with difficulty. Taking a deep breath, he sighed. It was a practiced gesture and he immediately felt shitty about it. Tensing with a rush of adrenaline, he tried to look her in the eye but couldn't hold the gaze. His eyes fell back to the water. "It just happened. I don't know how. I never meant to hurt you. I didn't even know it was going to happen. I thought it was just friendship. God, I'm a fuck up. Twelve years we've been married and I never. Shit. You don't know how fucking hard it's been these last four weeks. I've always told you everything. I wouldn't be now." He forced himself to look at her. Her large, brown eyes looked back at him but not in the way he expected. No anger, or even hurt, but curious. Her mouth was slightly parted. "I wouldn't now, but I have to. I have the clap. Gonorrhea. Not that serious, but you have to get on antibiotics too. I'm sorry, Jennie. You don't deserve this."

Her lips tightened. The brown eyes lost their focus on him as if looking at some object in the distance, then switched direction altogether, moving about as if she was watching a dragonfly in flight. Air expelled out of her mouth and with it a whisper, "Shit."

He continued his confession, his apology, his rationalization, pleading with himself as much as with her that he still loved her, their child, their marriage. He saw she listened, not knowing what she heard.

• • •

She called her gynecologist the next day, explaining to him that her husband was at a writers' conference and had gotten gonorrhea. That she needed a prescription. When finished with the call she went to him and said, "It's taken care of. At least medically. Just make sure you finish the whole prescription." They were the only harsh words she said to him all day. She even smiled after it. And later, on her way to bed, caressed his back when she passed him sitting at the desk. Goddamn you, he thought, seared by her understanding.

• • •

Jennie, Jennie, she kept hearing a voice call, not her own, yet not unfamiliar. It was rhythmic, but did not correspond with the beating of her heart. That rose from her chest, displaying itself in the undersides of her wrist, the soft flesh of her throat, her temples. No, the voice came from afar, buzzing from a distance, beating upon her eardrums, echoing faintly when it dissipated.

Hours before she heard him pacing the living room, and when he finally came to bed, falling heavily onto his side of the mattress, she waited, expecting him to realize she was not asleep. Long sighs rose and fell away into steady breathing and then the slight gurgling in his throat. How can you sleep! her thoughts screamed. She wanted to pound on his chest, rake his cheeks raw, make him confront the pain she felt. But she did not. Tears came slowly, with an effort. They mingled with the anger, diluting it, finally making her drowsy. But the voice was insistent and did not allow her to sleep, repeating, Jennie, Jennie, Jennie.

• • •

All day he wanted to talk to her, call her at work, know what she was feeling. Even when he and his four-year old son played baseball, his mind ran over imaginary conversations between Jennie and himself.

"What's the matter, Daddy?" Jonathan asked, his face displaying concern.

"Nothing," he answered, looking at the child with pangs of guilt, forcing himself to smile as he threw the plastic ball back to his son.

"Then why you looking like that, Daddy? Daddy, why you mad?"

"Just being silly, Johno. I'm not mad at you. I'm thinking about something else." The boy stared at him, the ball at his feet. Brown eyes, her eyes, their shape, color, expression.

"That's okay," his son told him and promptly went back to their game. Setting the ball on top of the batting tee. He could see Jonathan's concentration, then his fluid swing. Hours of time spent together developed that swing. Proper bat position, the step into the ball, transferring his weight, driving the ball with solid contact. David ran to the hit ball, and sprinted back toward Jonathan, who was rounding an imaginary base path, looking back over his shoulders at David coming at him. The boy lunged towards home plate, just a bare spot on the ground, worn free of grass from use. It was a good slide and Jonathan sprang back up onto his feet, looking to his father with excited eyes, exclaiming, "Safe!" throwing his arms wide in the proper gesture. David started to laugh and fell to his knees in front of the boy and they embraced, then fell to the ground in a tangle of arms and legs. Jonathan grabbed David's face, holding it between his palms and said, "Did you see that, Daddy? I hit that one *far!*"

"Yes, you did."

"That make you happy?" David tried to hug his son again but was pushed away, the boy scrambling back to his feet, grabbing the ball, saying, "Let's do it again."

• • •

For that one moment of the day he had been happy, but as he glowered at the blank sheet of paper, the memory served only as a yardstick for the depths of his depression. Jennie had been curt to him after she arrived home from work and he retreated to his desk. But he could not work. Instead he listened to his wife and son in the other room. Giggles, whispers, compliments from Jennie about how well Jonathan was doing with his letters. David thought, here I am, a writer, and the kid would grow up a fucking illiterate if it wasn't for her. Of course, this was not true.

He spent time with Jonathan, telling him stories. Mindstories, Jonathan called them. And he read to him a great deal. The two of them would traipse around the local library, finding new books to take home for the week. But self-lacerating admonishments were common for him during times of depression.

In a fit of rage he jammed his black, felt tip pen into the middle of his empty paper, piercing not only the paper, but the soft pine beneath. Rumpling the white sheet, he stared at the mar in the desk. Stupid, he thought. Stupid asshole. And as if to verify this he stabbed at the desk again and again, pocking the wood with small, blackstained holes. He snapped the pen in disgust and flung it into the wastebasket. Now the palm of his hand was colored with ink.

From Jonathan's bedroom he heard the melody of the music box they put on when either he or Jennie lay with their child to put him to sleep. A pang of melancholy hit him and he switched on the stereo, found a jazz station, and lit a cigarette. After taking two drags he crushed it out in the filled ashtray. Pulling another sheet of paper out of a drawer, he covered the damage he made with the pen and stared at the paper as he had done before. Starting to uncap a pen, he thought better of it. His head swam with bitter revulsion. *Poète manqué* floated from a cerebral depth, hanging upon his conscious thought like a strong taste on his palate. What shall I use to wash it away?

Fumbling within a bottom drawer he produced a wooden cigar box and placed it on the desk. A priest placing sacraments on the altar for communion. Opening the box, he checked several vials, each containing various types of Cannabis. Maui Wowie. Just the ticket. Placing the feathery bud on the whiteness of paper, he studied the hues of gold and green, a purplish vein, the crystalline quality of the resin. Index finger and thumb broke the bud into fine kernels and the aroma of earth and pine sap rose delicately into his nostrils. He took his time rolling the joint, spreading the dope evenly in the crease he made in the EZ Wider, then, with a practiced finesse, worked his fingers in unison. After licking the cigarette into shape he placed it on the paper to dry.

A wave of nausea hit. Probably the antibiotic, he thought, wincing in discomfort. It passed. At least it was working, his underwear remaining free of stains. Stemmed the rising tide of discharge from my prick, he thought; too bad it won't intercede with the salacious nature of my soul. He lit the joint and inhaled deeply. If I'm going to think like that I'm in bigger trouble than I thought. He pushed the sheet of paper aside.

It only took a few minutes for the marijuana to act. He took long, deep hits that seemed to swell in his lungs, and the lightheaded high turned into a siege of rolling euphoric waves. What stories his head conjured up! Of the swaggering, beggarman king, the vagabond iconoclast, the tortured sage—titles that depicted his moves about a private hell as a guide to the living for salvation. Writer martyr. Justification for his acts of perfidy. He rode upon these swells for almost an hour. The paper remained blank.

The only line he remembered was, *riding on the magic wave, in anticipation of the crash*. Depression intensified, and he sat, head in hands, treading water in open sea. He tried to cry, once even made his eyes water, but it was an act with actor's tears and he stopped trying. There was no reprieve from it, the ocean vast, no sign of land.

A screen door slammed, its noise just barely perceptible over the jazz. He turned off the stereo and listened. The house was quiet; then from the open window he heard shuffling feet upon the concrete driveway. After lighting a cigarette he got up and went outside.

She stood under the redbud tree, arms folded, shoulders hunched, as if fending off a chill. It was a swollen, humid night. Coming near, he stopped and watched her. Her eyes scanned the sky. A close Florida sky. Cloudless, it was a vast expanse of dark velvet, the stars bright. She did not acknowledge his presence, her only movement the rise and fall of her chest and the arms cradled upon it, her face luminous with a sheen of oil and sweat. Without a change of expression she told him, "What bothers me most is you didn't think of us. Didn't think of me. You said it just happened." Her head turned to look at him. Eyes hidden in shadow. Mouth, lips, teeth form articulation, the words, "Nothing *just* happens." A brief holding glare, then back to her star gaze.

Curious, he thought, I feel relieved, but still cheated. "Jennie …

"I don't know, David. I'll try."

He waited for more. Silence. The hanging sky. Beautiful. Mysterious. Oppressive. He left her to it, sulking back to his room. Went to finish the joint. Shut off the light. Sitting alone. Wanting only a sympathy high. The darkness.

He was sitting on the bed when she finally came in. Her hand came across to him. He held it. She slid up next to him. They held each other without speaking. Then they made love.

• • •

He became more aware of the activity of birds. At first it was not a conscious act, but he realized its source. Julie, the woman he had the affair with, gave him a feather the day after the act. He became touched by the gesture, though his initial reaction was a blend of feeling foolish and wondering if it was riddled with lice. I should trust my instincts, he thought. There was more to this: after an afternoon's swimming break from the conference, they explored an old abandoned church. Spring flood rains had cut a wash across a road, scarring a meadow and exposing the rock foundation of the church. They, Julie, David, and Larry traversed a plank across the created gorge, into the side entrance. The floor of this lower level was coated with a thick layer of dust. Julia's white gauze skirt got soiled at the hem. There were three large windows on the western wall, shafts of light falling into the body of the room. Alive with agitated motes. A fluttering panic beat against one of the panes. A sparrow trapped inside. With quick response Julia went to the bird and with sure hands cupped it within her palms. Both Larry and David wanted to see it, but Julia had already walked swiftly to the open door, freeing the bird to the air.

The symbolic gift of the feather brought this back to him, but he was confused by it. Like an illiterate trying to decipher a printed page staring at the words with such intensity, hoping their meaning would suddenly become clear, finding instead that the letters began to move, blur and blend together.

• • •

While Jonathan played on his swing set, and David read Roethke, a shrill call filled the air. David looked up and heard, then saw the wings. Just to the left of his son. White and brown striped. As the hawk traveled off, David noticed a flash of red in the bird's grasp. Later he looked it up in his bird book. Sharpshinned Hawk. Preys on small birds. A cardinal, he thought. He read about the osprey and other birds of prey.

...

It was a Saturday and Jennie took Jonathan to Daytona Beach. David had a job putting on a roof and she wanted to be out of the house. Jonathan loved the ocean, so he was excited.

Once there she tried to read a magazine while her son played at the water's edge. But she could not concentrate, so watched Jonathan play. First he alternately ran after and retreated from the waves, then played a game of chase with the sandpipers. He reminded her of a kitten. Finally he settled into building a sand castle. Scooping a handful of wet sand, the child allowed it to run out of his fist, creating a miniature mountain range. It intrigued Jennie and she went to the boy's side and started to build her own.

Her mind reeled from the blows she had suffered the past four days. Some self-inflicted. She almost did not go the the beach because of the reflection she studied in the mirror on this morning. Running her hands over the slight roll of flabby flesh on her stomach. Childbirth. The feeling of panic receded, especially when she arrived at the beach and viewed the other bodies roaming around. Her questions of what she had done to cause David to cheat on her receded as well. There were no answers.

Hell, she thought, I can't even sort out my feelings about all of this. She caught herself, on more than one occasion, seeing David's watchful eyes, attentive on her every reaction. And her silence. It made him suffer.

And while it was not a conscious act, it gave her a certain satisfaction. Not enough, though. Like sex without love. Was that it? Is that what it comes down to? This was not the answer, either. Was it the choice he made?

The only thing holding her together right now was the

memory of Michael, when she and David lived in Los Angeles. Before Jonathan was born. An actor who was working as a waiter. Met him at the laundromat of all places. She told David about him at the time. David was suspicious, but she told him, no, Michael's not like that. He's a friend. Her friend. And when she found out Michael really wanted more than that she was hurt. She told him to stop calling. Her choice. But still there was a sense of loss. It could have easily gone further. But she made a choice. What if?

She threw a clump of sand, destroying what she had made. Jonathan stared at her. "Why'd you do that, Mommy?" She did not answer him right away and he became insistent.

"Tide's coming in anyway. Come on, we're going home."

Jonathan grew upset that all his work would be washed away by the tide. "I don't want it!" he spit out after tears welled up in his eyes.

"You can't stop nature, Jonathan." She freed him of his tears by making a game of destroying his own castle by pitching handfuls of sand at it. Jonathan liked that. And after cleaning off their towels, after Jonathan took a last swim, Jennie dried him off. She packed up their beach gear, brushed off Jonathan's feet, buckled him into his seat, then started the car. As she pulled out she saw the last of their castles fall into an onrushing wave, leaving the surface smooth as it receded.

• • •

The physical labor freed him from thought. It was an emergency patch job. Doing a roof in Florida was January work. But the rainy season was coming, the leak had to be fixed, August sun or not.

"This flat should have been rolled, not shingled," Tom said. Tom was in his late fifties, a retired carpentry foreman from Pennsylvania. David liked working with him. He was taciturn, all business on the job. After work and a few Busch's, he told David stories. David respected, and more important to David, *liked* Tom.

Getting the old roof up was the rough part. A second set had been placed over the original shingles and the older ones were sodden. It was a bitch to get them off. Once down to the wood, after sweeping it clean and nailing the felt paper, they tarred the edge and laid down the first asphalt roll. Secured the edge with roofing nails, spacing each nail three inches apart. A lot of nails. The monotony of the task, the heat, and his already tired body allowed David to float as if drugged. The only breaks were for water and when they set a new chalk line. More tar just above the line. Place the roll, squaring it with the line. Nail it down.

When he got home he was exhausted. "Today was a real bastard," he said to Jennie. She smiled and nodded as she fixed dinner. He went directly to shower. His back and shoulders stung with sunburn even though he was tanned brown. After he turned off the hot water he stood under the cold shower. Jennie had to call him twice before he shut it off.

They ate in silence except for Jonathan, who told David about the beach with great animation. "And then you know what, Daddy? The tide came. To eat up my castle. But I didn't let it." The mischief in Jonathan's face made David smile. David glanced at Jennie. She was sitting back from her plate, her hand covering her own smile.

"What, Johno? How did you stop it."

"*I* knocked it down." Jonathan was proud of himself. "You know what else, Daddy?"

"What."

"You can't stop nature."

David started to laugh.

"Enough, Jonathan. Eat your dinner." Jennie's voice was sharp. Jonathan looked at his father.

"Eat, Johno," David told him. David poked at his own food. He wasn't hungry, only thirsty. "Pass the iced tea, please," he said to Jennie.

"Not much left," she said flatly, giving him the pitcher. The side of the pitcher was beaded with water.

"Dehydrated," David said, lifting his glass, chugging the tea.

"All right, Jonathan, enough! Time for your bath."

"Shower!"

"Bath!" She half dragged the boy to the bathroom.

The door was briskly closed behind them. David heard them talking quietly. Then the sound of the shower.

He usually helped Jennie clear off the dinner dishes, but he could hardly move. It was an effort to rise from the dinner table, grab a beer from the refrigerator, and stagger into the bedroom. He closed his eyes once he stretched out on the bed. The cold beer glided down his throat. The rhythmic percussion of hammers echoed inside his head, lulling him to sleep.

. . .

"Whoa!" he spit out, heart racing, breath short. His eyes were blinded in an attempt to adjust to the light in the bedroom. When he finally realized where he was, he found himself sitting up in bed, left leg on the floor. Looking to his right he saw Jennie sitting on the bed too, though she was on top the bedcovers. "What is it? Jonathan? What?"

"No. Jonathan's fine."

Then he saw her scowl. Set jaw. "What then?"

"You know."

"Shit." He flopped back down on the bed. His worn out body made it feel as if he were wearing wet clothes, anchoring him to the mattress. Anger rose in him, the only emotion he could show in times of stress. He tried to control it. "This couldn't wait until morning?" Measured words.

"I couldn't spend another sleepless night while you saw wood."

"Jesusfuckinchrist! Goddamn son of a bitch! For Godsake, I just worked ten fucking hours."

"To hell with that! I'm not going to suffer while you snore."

"And not pencilpushing hours! Ten fucking hours in the hot sun! Ripping off a roof! What do you want from me?"

"I want to be done with this one way or another!"

"I almost passed the fuck out twice."

"You're acting like this is my fault, my doing!"

"What the hell difference does that make?"

"Will you let me finish!"

"Fine. Sure. Go ahead."

She sat in silence for a moment trying to collect her thoughts. Almost in reflex she found herself saying, "I know what I wanted to say, but you interrupted."

"Go ahead. Floor's yours. God knows you've got my attention."

"You bastard."

"That's right. That's what I am. Why don't you try for A1 prick too. Lousy bastard that cheats on his wife. A wife that's given him everything. Sacrificed everything. For him. And what is he? Oh, he's a writer. Well, what does he do, really? My own fucking family can tell you that. *Bum* is what they'd tell you."

"Stop it. I hate it when you wallow in your self pity."

"And Jennie. Sweet Jennie. Everyone loves Jennie. Poor Jennie, they say. Perfect Jennie. Do you know what it's like to live with that? For Godsakes, I've had to live up to my perfect older brother. Oh yes, Carl's in the Air Force. A flight commander. David? He's still writing, but now he's at least going for a degree. At least he'll be able to teach. Perfect brother and now a perfect wife. I can't deal with it!"

"Don't lay that on me, David! You know I don't feel that way!"

"What do you want from me!" he screamed.

"I want you to think about me!"

"Goddamn it, Jennie, goddamn it. They're right. I can't work. I try, but no words come," he said, his voice suddenly quiet, almost whispers.

"I'm having a tough time, David. I don't know."

"Don't know what!" he was shouting again. "You want out? Go! Get the fuck out!" He was up now, stalking toward her. Grabbing her by the back of the neck, forcing her up off the bed, pushing her toward the door.

"Maybe I will!"

The fist flew past her head, burying itself in the wall.

Jennie ran into the night, away from him.

• • •

She heard the screen door open and close. Footfalls.

"Jennie," came the soft voice of contrition. "I'm sorry. I know that's not enough, but I'll try, really try. But you've got to try, too. You're sitting with a pat hand, Jen. Hell, I don't have any cards at all, and maybe that's the way it should be. I need us to be whole again." Shuffling feet. "That's what I wanted to say." He turned to leave.

"Who the hell do you think you are? You blow up, spit out your guts. And now you say you're sorry. It doesn't make it, David. *I* have all the cards? If you had made the right choice we wouldn't be playing this game. And for your information it's not a game. It's our lives. Did you hear me? *Our* lives. Don't flatter yourself. Sacrifice for you? No, no. Do you remember when I wanted a baby? Did you go back to work just for me? It was for *us*. Don't be so egocentric. And don't look for pity, David.

"You hurt me. But you hurt yourself too. You want me to forgive you? You can't forgive yourself. I know you, David. For Godsake we've grown up together. We learned how to make love together. We learned how to trust.

"It was just a fuck for her. She gained a night of pleasure. You're the one who lost something, David.

"We all make choices." She looked away from his shadowed figure, out into the night, to the moonlight bouncing off the lake across the street. She still felt angry, hurt, but better. "I'll be in in a while," she told him.

• • •

He sat on the bed in the dark room, knees hunched up against his chest. A glaze of moonglow plastered the back of his shoulders a resplendent blue. He started to speak as soon as she settled under the covers. "When I was five, in the hospital, for my first operation ..."

"On your eyes," she said, acknowledging a history she knew well. She remembered it was a hospital in New York City.

"Yes. The doctors and nurses told my parents when they came to visit me they had to wait out in the hall. That I made too much of a fuss when they left and it would be better to keep me calm. So they did. I remember looking out at the street every day. The crowds streaming by. I tried to find my parents' faces in the crowd, but I was up too high. I thought they left me. Forever."

They both fell silent for a time.

"You never told me that part of the story before."

"You keep that feeling away from me." He was crying now. She got out from beneath the blanket and took him in her arms. She felt her heart beat when she pressed against his flesh. Felt his tears strike her arm.

• • •

Three days later, in the early evening, she came home from work to find him at the desk.

"Where's Jonathan?"

"Late nap. We went to the movies." He nodded toward a pile of papers on the desk.

"What's this?"

"Finished it about an hour ago. Been working on it for the past couple of days."

He listened to music while she read, but could not stand it for long. He went outside and hit plastic golf balls with a nine iron. Hearing the screen door shut, he waited until she called out to him. He walked over to the carport where she stood. "Well?"

"It's good, David. I like it a lot." He smiled. "Except for the title. `A Child's Prayer'?"

His smile turned sheepish. "I sort of feel the same way. But the story. You like the story?"

"Yes, David." She watched him think, his head down, staring intently at his feet. And then she noticed something she'd seen so many times, and it almost made her laugh. David had a habit of running his fingertips across the tip of his thumbs when he was nervous or actively thinking. A frenzy of flight at first, as if he were trying to rub away some dirt, then the slow, thorough caress, as if to make sure he would have a true grip on whatever came into his hands. "Think about the title, David," she said, "but it's a good story."

He looked up at her. "Something to work on, right?"

On impulse she leaned over to kiss her husband on his lips. It wasn't a passionate kiss, but a serious, caring one. She then tweaked his nose and headed into the house, holding the papers in a tight grip by her side.

David turned and headed toward his practice balls. His golf swing suddenly felt fluid and right. His shots started to land closer to the target in his mind.

Mark Hillringhouse

Running Around

It wasn't tripping on acid
stationed at the flame broiler
mixing up the meat with the buns at Burger King
watching as the blackened buns burst into flame.

And it wasn't stocking shelves
in the supermarket hiding from the manager
ripping open boxes of cookies.

And it wasn't hauling bags of mail
off the back ends of trucks
killing boredom in the post office
opening letters, stealing apples from fruit shipments;

or climbing up ladders
with 80-pound packs of shingles
hammering nails in the 90-degree heat;

or sitting alone
in a security booth trying to stay awake
with a stack of books;

or getting drunk on the beer
the second shift left and finding myself unconscious
on the restroom floor, the foreman yelling:
I had left the bay doors open.

And it wasn't breathing in toxic fumes
on the paint conveyor belt,
or the long hours standing on cold cement floors
punching out metal slugs.

And it wasn't when unemployment ran out,
and a federal work program sent me to the library
to collect overdue library books,
and knowing how stupid the job looked,
I went fishing after punching in
until I got fired.

And it wasn't sitting in a cubicle
on the fortieth floor making telemarketing calls;
or working in a bookstore
hoarding volumes of poetry,
reading in a corner while getting stoned;

or working as a house painter
and drinking all the profits,
or making drinks all night at a club
and falling in love with all the waitresses,
and sleeping all day.

No, it wasn't the odd jobs
that made me feel sorry for things I did,
and it wasn't when I deserted my first wife
and left her stranded in a motel out west,
until I broke down by the side of the road
in the middle of Montana.

No, it was sleeping with my best friend's girlfriend
one night while he was away
because she must have told him
about our first kiss

thinking no one else existed
except the two of us
alone in our own deep winter,
when I lost him
and he lost her
and all of us lost each other.

Thomas E. Kennedy

That Night on the Farm

The season is spring, the setting Celtic, the year 1978, the day a rare Dublin Saturday with sunlight glinting on the Liffey as it flows beneath the O'Connell Street Bridge. A tinker girl holding a baby with soot-smudged face in her shawl sits against the abutment, shaking a paper cup. You drop a five p. coin into the cup and decide to change direction. You were headed north over the bridge, but instead follow your feet south across the river in search of what the day might offer.

You have a room at Trinity, in Building 38, the very room in which J. P. Donleavy stayed when he studied there under the G.I. Bill in the '40s, and you have the remainder of Saturday and Sunday morning free, your conference having ended the night before. The flight back to Copenhagen was cheaper if you stayed the weekend, even with the extra expense of lodging and meals.

You have an idea for the perfect gift for your wife and turn toward Nassau Street, past the sculpture of Molly Malone with her wheelbarrow ("The Tart with the Cart"), follow along the grey stone wall of Trinity to Merrion Square, turn left, then left again to No. 1 Lincoln Place, and are cheered to see that Sweny's Chemist is still open. You let yourself into the little shop and browse among the wares on display, finding just what you hoped you might: a fist-sized lump of Bronnley's lemon soap, wrapped in tissue. You lift it to your nose and sniff the lemony aroma, imagining your way back to June 16th, 1904, the fictional day when Leopold Bloom bought just the same soap from just this same shop for his wife, Molly, even as he knew she was preparing to commit adultery with Blazes Boylon. Or was it for Molly? Seems he used it for other purposes. Not important—tell the story that way.

"Is it for herself?" asks the twinkly-eyed old woman from behind the ancient wooden desk, and you smile, nod, pay, and store the lump of tissue-wrapped soap in your hip pocket in honor of Poldy, poor peaceful contemplative cuckold Jew.

On the street, you pause, staring across at Kennedy's Public House and wonder what your wife will make of your giving her a bar of soap famous for having been given to the adulteress Molly. But the soap was a symbol of Leopold's great love for Molly, despite all. No need to go into the details; she'll love it.

Now it is nearing noon, soon lunchtime, but your belly is still content from breakfast at Trinity's Buttery: eggs, rashers and sausage, black and white pudding, fried mushroom and tomato, baked beans and toast. All that was lacking was a pint, which you will soon remedy.

Your shoes walk you riverward again, along Duke, past The Duke and The Bailey and Davy Byrnes, left on Grafton past Bewley's, right on Harry Street past McDaid's, and left past the Brazen Arms. All fine public houses, but there's another you have thought of that you'd like to visit, through Dame Court, across Dame Street, down Temple Lane, you enter the Temple Bar in Temple Bar, where you can sit out in the open sunny courtyard with your pint of the black stuff and, with luck, might wrangle a glass of potjeen from the barman.

You take a high stool alongside a barrel and contemplate the antique tin signs mounted on the walls, advertising Poser's Whiskey, Bagot's Hutton & Co. Fine Old Whiskey/Murphy's/From the Wood that's Good, Bulmer's: Nothing Added but Time, Crested Ten: John Jameson & Son, Murphy's Extra Stout: On Draught and In Bottle, Lady's Well Brewery-Cork, Cantwell's Café au lait ... *Whiskey, it keepeth the reason from stifling.*

You quaff your black stuff and, sighing, wipe your mouth with the back of your hand, ready for another, and as you rise you notice a young woman seated just around the corner of a wooden pillar, dark-haired and blue-eyed, lovely combination, wearing tight faded jeans and a tee shirt of ponderous contours. She is reading

The New Yorker and nursing the skimpy remains of a pint of lager.

"*New Yorker!*" you exclaim. "Makes me homesick."

"For New York?"

"Born and raised there." You neglect to specify in Queens. "Yourself?"

"Cleveland."

"Largest Slovenian population in the world outside of Slovenia."

She sits up in her chair, affording a fine view of her allurements, blushing with what appears to be pleasure. "Lived there all my life, and I didn't know that!"

"Just shtick with me, kid," you say. "You'll learn lots you didn't know."

She laughs merrily, and you can see how young she is, and you wonder what in the world you are doing, but choose not to pursue that particular question just now, not just yet. Instead, you say, "Another pint?"

She looks at her glass as though she hadn't noticed it was empty; then: "Sure. Okay. Thanks."

Inside, the barman, with a twisted nose and a sweet smile, looks at you and barks, "Talk to me!"

You order a pint of harp and another of the black stuff, spot a sign offering half a dozen river oysters for a pittance and order them, too. You pay, but keep your wallet out. "You know what—I'd also like two small potjeens."

"If it's potjeen you're after you'll have to go to the Garda. They've confiscated it all."

You lean close across the bar, speak softly, "My girl and I have to go back later today, and we haven't even tasted it and would so very much like to. Could you help us?"

"The two of you come over together, did you?" he says with a smirk.

You smile, shrug.

He steps away from the bar and returns with a tumblerful of clear spirit which he sets before you.

"How much do I owe you?" you ask.

"Can't sell it to you. Illegal."

You put a handful of coins on the bar, and he says, "That's grand. I'll bring your oysters out to you."

"Won't we have a lovely time," you say to the girl, balancing the three glasses over the threshold to the courtyard, "drinking whiskey gin and wine, on Coronation day."

The barman comes out afterwards and lays a plate of half shells on the barrel head, along with brown bread and butter. "Get it down your necks now," he says, "it's good for you."

The young woman looks skeptically at the oysters. You squeeze on lemon, scoop one off the shell on the blade of the knife, cutting the muscle free beneath the hinge, and mouth it down, drink the juice from the shell and wash it back with potjeen. Then you scoop another onto the blade and hold it out to her, cupping your free hand beneath it. Her eyes meet yours. She looks at the cup of your left, turns your hand in hers and looks at the ring. "What?" she asks. "You're married?"

"Yes," you say and meet her gaze, still holding the oyster on the blade. She studies you for a moment, a smile pursing her lips. Then she opens her mouth and delivers it to you for the oyster. She closes her eyes, smiling, hums with pleasure, and you hold the glass of potjeen to her.

"Enhances the taste," you say and lean forward to kiss her.

She is twenty-one years old, thirteen years your junior. She is in her last year at the American College of Dublin on Merrion Square. She dances ballet. Neither of you again mentions the fact that you are married. You take her back to Trinity with you, through the brick portal where a sign says, "Cyclists Dismount," and across the cobblestoned square to Building 38 and into your high-ceilinged, tall-windowed room where you undress and admire one another and partake of each other's bodies. Then you share the sharp cheddar and stilton and biscuits and burgundy remaining in your larder, and she produces a joint which you smoke before another, slower partaking of one another. You marvel at the block-like structure of her feet, misshapen from years of dancing ballet.

A little before ten, she says she has to leave if she is to make curfew, kisses your mouth, takes one final smiling look into your eyes and is gone. No names, no addresses, no phone numbers.

The room has grown dark through the afternoon and evening. She left a roach in the ashtray using your tie clasp as a roach clip, you get three small hits out of it and lie on the bed with your fingers over your mouth. They smell of lemon and oyster and cunt, and as your exhileration begins to fade, you try to remember a question that had popped into your head earlier, but has been eluding you all day.

The flight to Copenhagen next day is on Aer Lingus. You sit in the back rows, where you can smoke, and you drink vodka for the two hours it takes back to Kastrup, turning the Bronnley's lemon soap over and over in your hands, its fresh, innocent scent lifting to your nose.

You are home by five p.m. Your wife greets you with a kiss, sniffs, says, "Vodka."

"I had one on the plane."

She has made fresh liver paste and baked rye bread for dinner —things she knows you love. She is delighted with the lemon soap, which you tell her Leopold bought for Molly in 1904. You do not tell the details of what Molly did that day while Leopold wandered through Dublin. You tell the story of your own week in that city, the Joyce conference, and of the nice long walk you took on your free day. You tell it just as it happened, though you eliminate one character from the cast.

You also bought a full bottle of Carte Noir from duty free, and your wife makes coffee and has a little bakery box of petit fours which you take on the balcony to your apartment which looks down the hilly street to the castle gardens. The sky is still light at this time of year. You can see the green copper towers of the castle, and you toast with your snifters and smoke cigarettes and she smells her hands, which she has washed with Bronnley's lemon soap, and hums with pleasure at the smell, and then the two of you fall silent.

You are thinking dangerous thoughts that you do not wish to think. You think about the four years of your marriage, the three apartments the two of you have lived in, each one a little better than the last. You think about the wild years you lived before you left New York and how you had believed you'd left all that behind. You think about how easily this thing happened yesterday, how you made it happen, no one to blame but yourself, and you did it without a thought. First chance you really had in four years, and you grabbed it without a thought, went directly to action. Is that what your marriage vows are worth? you wonder.

You caution yourself not to be rash, not to tell her, but you fear the whole story tells itself on your lying, adulterous face.

Your wife sits in shadow on the balcony, barely visible in the flickering of the dish of votive candles she has lit on the table between you. It occurs to you how quiet she has been since you got home, how quiet and loving. Which is not really like her. She is not the tender-hearted sort, is a professional woman, has to make it in a man's world.

She reaches for the Carte Noir. "May I?" she asks, holding it over her empty snifter.

That's not like her either. You nod. "Of course."

She tops you up, then pours for herself, re-corks the bottle and says, "Henrik stopped by."

"Henrik?"

"You remember, our neighbor from the north side? The guy who was married to the Polish woman?"

"Oh, Henrik. Haven't seen him in years. How is he? What'd he want?"

"I had to ask him to leave."

"Really? Why?"

She inhales deeply. "There's something I have to tell you. I hope you will listen all the way before you react."

You stare at her. Then she is telling you about something that happened more than three years ago, not a year after you married.

She reminds you of the time you and she went to a summer party at a farm on Funen. The dinner was held in a renovated barn. There were many guests. The girl seated beside you was flirting, and you danced a couple of times with her, and your wife was tipsy and got furious and stormed out into the fields, and you couldn't find her. You sat alone on a bench and felt miserable. Nothing had happened with the girl—you only danced with her, but you were sad that you'd made your wife, your new bride, jealous and unhappy. So you sat on the bench, waiting for her to return, and drank bottles of beer in the steeping dusk while people danced in the barn and ran around the farmyard, laughing and kissing and drinking green bottles of beer, and rock blasted from the big speakers that had been set up.

Finally your wife showed up and apologized for getting so jealous, and you went up to the room you'd been given—a room you shared, you remember now, with Henrik and his Polish wife. The Polish wife had gone to bed early, and now Henrik was there with her, too, and they were making love, and you and your wife crawled into a sleeping bag and made love, too. It was kind of piquant, making love in the same room with the other couple.

"Where were you all that time you were gone?" you ask now. "I never figured that out. You were gone for two or three hours."

"I was with Henrik," she says. "I was drunk." She lowers her eyes. "He fucked me." She looks at your face again. "I'm laying my cards on the table and hoping you will forgive me."

"What did he want when he came by now?"

"He's called me a couple of times since that night, wanted to see me. I told him it was out of the question. He called again on Saturday and wanted to come over, but I told him you were away, and it was out of the question. He suggested that you could sleep with his wife."

"Is that what you want?"

"Of course not! I hung up on him, I was so pissed off, and he just came over. I didn't let him in. I told him to go away. I'm hoping that telling you about this, that you can forgive me."

You reach for the Carte Noir and refill your glass, reach to pour for her, light a cigarette.

"Will you forgive me?" she asks. "I took the chance of telling you. I hoped we could wipe the slate clean."

"Just let me absorb this first, okay?"

"When a person asks for forgiveness," she says, "it's *cheap* not to give it." You can hear that she's getting mad now, which she has no grounds to. You have no grounds to be righteous either, but this has all flooded in on you, and you have to absorb it. You cannot help but think of the fact that when you and she made love that night on the farm that Henrik's cock had been there first. You wonder if he came in her, if she at least washed herself. You think about the fact that Henrik and *his* wife were making love in the same room as the two of you and what was he thinking about as he fucked his wife and you fucked yours, that he had been there first that night, and you were getting sloppy seconds?

What right do you have?

You shield your eyes with your palm and say, "It's okay. I forgive you. I just need time to absorb this."

"Come to bed," she says. "Make love to me."

"Please, I need a little time. You go in. I'll be in in a while. Let me smoke a cigarette and absorb this."

"Don't be like that," she says and stubs out her own cigarette. "Let's put this behind us. Forgive and forget. Don't be cheap."

"I can't make love to you right at this minute. I need a little time. Please, just go in. I'll be in later."

"Fuck you," she says, and her feet are hard across the floor. The bedroom door slams after her.

You stand by the railing of the little balcony and smoke another cigarette, looking out at the dim gloamy evening like a dusky land of dreams. You flip your cigarette into the darkness and go in to the bathroom. The lemon soap is still wet in the soap dish on the sink. You can smell it. You brush your teeth, wash your hands and face with the soap, stand in the hall looking at the bedroom door, decide to have another cognac and a cigarette.

From your chair on the balcony, you can see the bedroom door. You wonder if you have waited too long, ruined something. You think about Henrik, whose face you cannot quite recall, a tallish skinny guy, try to picture him fucking her in the fields. Now you're getting mad, but remember then what you were doing yesterday. It seems strange that the pleasures of that Saturday have now lost their luster. Maybe it's not too late to go in to her, but you don't rise. Not yet. You just want to run it through your mind one more time, try to think it all through clearly.

Walter Cummins

Hide & Seek

Roger aimed his Nikon digital, quickly snapping one shot after another before the layers of purple-red sunset vanished. Paul hung a propane lantern from an aluminum pole behind the adults' table. The children were eating by themselves off at another table. Marilyn, Roger's wife, and Eleanor, Paul's wife, had served the food—sizzling ham steaks with fresh corn and snap beans bought at a vegetable stand a hundred miles back. Craig and Colette, new to the campground, immediately friendly, contributed the wine, two bottles of Bordeaux produced from their orange rucksack.

Roger zoomed in on Colette, pretending to focus, as if taking a picture. When Eleanor seemed to notice, he capped the lens and studied the sky, first closing his left eye, then his right.

Eleanor and Marilyn were sitting on a redwood bench, Paul standing behind Marilyn as he tended the grill, while Craig and Colette sprawled on the ground, his head pillowed on her stomach, her head propped against the rucksack. The adults drank the wine from plastic cups. The older children popped open soda cans, spraying each other with fizz; the young ones chased fireflies.

A campfire log collapsed, sending up a shower of sparks.

"This is almost like candlelight," Eleanor said.

"Better!" Marilyn turned to Paul with a smile. He smiled back.

Roger looked through the camera again, swinging back and forth from Marilyn to Eleanor, Eleanor to Marilyn, pausing on Marilyn before he took the picture. Paul, his best friend for many years, blurred in the background.

Marilyn was a small woman, spidery thin, with a pug nose and close-cropped curls. She sat hunched, wrapped arms tight around her knees as if trying to pull herself into a tight ball. Eleanor, though only medium height, seemed tall in comparison, her auburn hair brushed back into a tight frame for a face made formal by silver-rimmed glasses. Both Roger and Paul were trim, clean-featured men who looked right in whatever clothes they wore, from business suits to their Orvis camping outfits. Any stranger could tell the couples enjoyed comfortable lives.

The men had picked the campsite from a map because it seemed so isolated, five miles deep in the woods off a single-lane dirt road. Paul towed a pop-up camper and Roger pitched a 12 by 15 cabin tent. For two weeks the families had been sharing food, blankets, and fishing gear, the cooking and the cleaning up.

Craig and Colette had arrived at the campsite the previous night, long after dark, emerging into the sunrise from the cocoon of a nylon tent, waving to Roger as he gathered kindling to start a coffee fire. They said they had been traveling all summer on a motorcycle, although, like the other couples, they were in their late thirties. Craig was either growing a reddishblond beard or was lazy about shaving. Colette, tall and fullbodied, dressed in cutoff jeans and a man's tee shirt. Her breasts hung low and widespread, nipples large and dark against the white cotton. Roger saw that Eleanor didn't approve of her, but he couldn't read Marilyn's reaction, suspecting his wife's show of friendliness.

After the meal Paul retrieved a sixpack chilling in the river and snapped open a can for each of them. Craig threw his head back and drained his in several long gulps. When he wiped his mouth with the back of his hand, Marilyn broke the silence, looking straight at Craig. "Where else have you been?"

Craig crushed his can with his fist and tossed it into the fire. "Ontario, the Michigan peninsula, the Adirondacks, Acadia."

"All on a motorcycle?" Eleanor said.

"Sure. Why not?"

"How do you shop?"

"We avoid cans and bottles," Colette said, her voice husky, "anything heavy. Except the wine. And we eat what's around us in the woods.   Berries, roots. Craig's very good at knowing what's edible."

Their motorcycle had a mud-splattered license plate. Paul asked where they were from.

"We're in transit," Colette told him.

"To where?"

"Possibly Vermont. Maybe upstate New York."

"Don't you know?"

"We're not definite."

"Won't you have to decide soon?" Paul said.

Colette shrugged. "Before the first snow."

"Isn't a motorcycle bad for your kidneys?" Eleanor winced. "All that bouncing around."

"In a car," Craig said, speaking slowly as if plucking thoughts from the air, "you're all sealed in. Watching pictures flash by the windows. But on a bike you're really part of the landscape. You're attuned to everything around you."

The first impression Craig gave with his stubbled face, his torn workshirt and filthy dungarees, was that of a vagrant, the word Paul had whispered to Roger. But when he spoke, his words soft, his enunciation clear, he seemed educated.

"I'd be scared to death to be all exposed like that." Eleanor turned up her shirt collar, rolled down the sleeves.

"What's your work, Craig?" Paul asked.

Craig looked up and studied Paul closely, then stared at Roger with the same intensity. "Do you know that you two look alike?"

"Everybody says that," Eleanor offered. "Like brothers."

"But they're not." Marilyn grinned as if that pleased her.

"They're very good friends," Eleanor insisted.

"But you and Marilyn are quite different," Craig said. He framed his hands and turned from one to the other.

"How long have you all known each other?" Colette asked.

"Fifteen years," Eleanor said, proud of the number.

"Our first children were born in the same month, just twelve days apart," Marilyn added.

"Then you must all be very close," Colette said, her voice trilling on the "very."

"We're like one family." Eleanor looked to Marilyn for confirmation.

Craig smiled at them both. "It's very nice to have such dear old friends," he said.

"We share each other's memories," Paul said. Roger nodded.

"There's a comfort," Marilyn said, "in knowing someone else has the same experiences. It's like being able to verify your life through them."

"What about *you*," Eleanor asked. "Don't you feel sad about moving, parting from old friends?"

"We never stay in one place for long," Colette said.

"But when you're talking to people like us," Marilyn said, "don't you feel that you're missing something?"

Colette shrugged. "You can't have everything."

Roger felt sure she was mocking them.

Eleanor looked at her watch. "My God! We should be cleaning up." She yelled over to the children to help clear the tables. They whined that they were playing.

"Now!" Paul ordered.

"Listen to Eleanor," Roger said, glancing at Colette.

The children worked quickly, dumping paper plates, the soda and beer cans, the wine bottles into a plastic garbage bag. Then they began a spontaneous game of hide and seek under the glow of the half moon. "Don't go far," Marilyn warned. "Stay in sight of the fire."

Shivering in the night breeze, she went into the camper for a sweater and brought one back for Eleanor. Colette said she wasn't cold, but Roger could see the goosebumps on her arms, the taut points of her nipples.

"Let's play too," Craig said.

"Play what?" Marilyn asked.

"Hide and seek of course."

"I haven't done that in twenty-five years," Paul said.

"Why not?"

Paul shrugged. "It's for kids."

"One of the advantages of being an adult," Craig said, "is that you can do anything you like."

Roger looked at Colette's broad pelvis. "I'm all for it," he said.

Eleanor began to shake her head, but Paul spoke first. "Why not? We're on vacation."

Paul argued that Craig should be it because the game had been his idea. Craig laughed and accepted. He cradled his head on the table and began to count slowly to one hundred. The others just watched until Colette asked, "Isn't anyone going to hide?" They scattered back into the trees, away from the children.

Roger watched Colette's movements and took a roundabout route to follow her down toward the launching ramp at the river where she crouched among the aluminum canoes. Paul caught Marilyn's hand and led her through a tangle of low sweeping branches to the base of a great pine tree. Eleanor turned an anxious circle and bolted into the shadows of her camper.

Craig counted loud warning numbers that rang out through the woods: "... 98, 99, 100. Here I come. Into your secret places."

"It's nice here," Marilyn whispered to Paul. "Smell the trees."

"There's nothing like a bed of pine needles," he said.

"Do you think Craig will find us?"

"Never. We're too shrewd for him."

Roger crept up to Colette and pretended surprise when he saw her. "We've picked the same spot," he said. "We must think alike."

"I'm sure we have the same ideas about some things."

He stretched out beside her between the canoes. "We ought to keep our heads down so Craig can't see us."

"Don't worry. He won't look very hard."

"Why not?"

"Craig isn't a serious person."

"Are you?"

"Very rarely."

Even with her sweater Eleanor was cold under the camper.

She hugged her arms to her chest and lay on her side with her knees pulled up toward her middle. She felt like an idiot, annoyed that Paul hadn't stayed close. What if one of the children should see her? Craig skipped about the clearing, chanting their names as if they were lost kittens. Once he passed so close Eleanor could have reached out and touched his shoe.

Paul held Marilyn's hand. It was the first time he had done so in all the years they had known each other, but she was not surprised. She wondered what it would feel like to slide closer and put her head on his shoulder.

"Are Roger and I really so much alike?" he asked her.

"Sometimes I mistake you from a distance."

"Up close is what matters."

"Inside," she said.

"Are we the same inside?"

It struck her that she didn't really know.

He squeezed her hand. "But we know we like each other."

"Yes, we do." She squeezed back.

Colette rolled over and looked up at the stars. Roger braced his chin in his palm to watch her chest rise and fall with each breath. Strands of her tangled hair glowed in the moonlight. When she did not speak, he became uneasy. "Do you want me to hide somewhere else?"

"Should I?"

"I was afraid I might be cramping you."

"I'll let you know."

Eleanor watched Craig light a cigarette as he moved to the edge of the trees. When he disappeared into the darkness, she felt totally alone and wanted the others with her, the children too, all pressed in the tight space under the camper, warming the night with their closeness.

"Are you glad to be away from them?" Marilyn asked Paul.

"Craig and Colette?"

She didn't answer.

"You're right," Paul said. "It's nice here."

A clatter of footsteps slapped across the river bridge, childish squeals. Roger squeezed his body against the ground. When Colette started to speak, he touched a finger to her lips. She bit it with a quick snap and he jerked away.

Craig emerged from the darkness and crossed the clearing directly to the camper; he opened the door and climbed inside. Eleanor heard the creak of springs from the axle beside her as he stretched out on one of the bunks. For a moment she wanted to pound the metal bottom with her fists, but held back, afraid to make such a disturbing noise.

"We could run away," Paul told Marilyn.

"How?"

"Steal Craig and Colette's motorcycle and roar off into the night."

"How would we live?"

"I'd develop Craig's sense for what's edible."

"And the children?"

"They'd stay with Roger and Eleanor?"

"Together?"

"Would it matter?"

"Maybe Roger will run off with Eleanor first," Marilyn said.

"Highly unlikely."

"Highly."

They muffled laughter with their hands.

"What's our best argument for running off?" Marilyn asked.

"You'd finally learn how I'm different from Roger."

Tentatively, Roger returned his finger to Colette's lips. But this time she opened her mouth. He was on her in an instant, straddling her thighs with his legs, plunging his hand beneath the tee shirt.

One of the children poked his head under the trailer, startled to see Eleanor. "Go away," she hissed. "I'm hiding too."

"Why are you so quiet?" Paul asked Marilyn. "Making up your mind?"

"I'm trying to imagine what it would be like to run away with you on a motorcycle."

"How would it be?"

"Fun. For a while."

"Then what?"

"You'd miss Eleanor and I'd miss Roger."

"Are you so sure?"

"I have to believe that."

"Why?"

"If I didn't all our lives would fall apart. We'd drown in a chaos of possibilities."

Roger put his lips on Colette's ear, then moved his mouth to hers. She yielded for several seconds, then raked his arm with her fingernails. At the sudden stinging pain, he wondered how he would explain the scratches to the others.

Eleanor sneezed, an explosion in the still night. Then she sneezed again and decided she wasn't going to risk a bad cold just for a childish game. She pulled herself out into the open and climbed into the camper.

Craig shined a flashlight in her eyes. "So you've finally decided to come out."

"Why aren't you looking for the others?"

"I know where they are."

"Then you should go catch them."

Craig turned the light on his soft smile. "I already have."

Editors

Walter Cummins has published more than 100 stories in such magazines as *Kansas Quarterly, New Letters, Other Voices, Crosscurrents, Florida Review, South Carolina Review, Green Hills Literary Lantern, Virginia Quarterly Review, Bellevue Literary Review, Valpariaso Fiction Review*, and *Confrontation*, and on the Internet. His story collections are titled *Witness, Where We Live, Local Music, The End of the Circle, The Lost Ones*, and *Habitat: Stories of Bent Realism*. He also has published novels, memoirs, essays, articles, and reviews. With Thomas E. Kennedy, he is co-publisher of Serving House Books.

Thomas E Kennedy has published novels, story and essay collections, books of literary criticism and of translation, and many anthologies (several co-edited with Walter Cummins). His most recent books include the novels of his *Copenhagen Quartet* being published world-wide by Bloomsbury—four independent novels about the seasons and souls of the Danish capital, each set in a different season and written in a different style (www.CopenhagenQuartet.com and www.thomasekennedy.com). The fourth, *Beneath the Neon Egg*, will appear in 2014, and the third. *Kerrigan in Copenhagen*, was an Editor's Choice selection in the Sunday *New York Times Book Review*. In 2012, New American Press published his *Getting Lucky: New & Selected Stories, 1982-2012*. Kennedy's stories, essays, and translations from the Danish appear regularly in American periodicals and have won O. Henry and Pushcart Prizes as well as a National Magazine Award in 2013.

Contributors

Renée Ashley is the author of five volumes of poetry (*Because I Am the Shore I Want to Be the Sea,* Subito Press, Univ. of Colorado—Boulder; *Basic Heart,* X. J. Kennedy Poetry Prize, Texas Review Press; *The Various Reasons of Light; The Revisionist's Dream; Salt,* Brittingham Prize in Poetry, Univ. of Wisconsin Press), two chapbooks (*The Verbs of Desiring,* New American Press Chapbook Prize, and *The Museum of Lost Wings,* Hill-Stead Museum Sunken Garden Poetry Competition) and a novel (*Someplace Like This),* as well as numerous essays and reviews.

Dennis F. Bormann has an MFA in Creative Writing from Vermont College and a Ph.D. in English from Oklahoma State. Teaching literature and creative writing at Claflin University, Bormann has been a fiction editor for *Midlands Review, Cimarron Review, Short Story,* and currently for Main Street Rag's literary magazine. His short novel, *Airboat,* was published by MSR in August 2011. Along with Stephen Taylor, Bormann also edited an anthology for MSR based on Sports titled *Suicidally Beautiful.*

Rebecca Chace is the author of: *Leaving Rock Harbor* (novel): "Editor's Choice" *New York Times Book Review,* finalist for the 2010 New England Book Award; *Chautauqua Summer* (memoir): *New York Times Book Review* "Notable Book", "Editor's Choice"; *Capture the Flag* (novel) Ms. Chace adapted for the screen with director Lisanne Skyler; the Showtime Tony Cox Screenwriting Award (Short Film), Nantucket Film Festival, 2010. She has written for the *New York Times Magazine, New York Times Book Review,* the *Huffington Post,* NPR's *All Things Considered,* and other publications. She is an assistant professor of creative writing at Fairleigh Dickinson University and a 2014 recipient of the Grace Paley Fiction Fellowship at the Vermont Studio Center.

Flower Conroy's chapbook, "Escape to Nowhere," was first runner-up for the Ronald Wardall Poetry Prize, and was published by Rain Mountain Press. Her second chapbook, "Controlled Burn," was first runner-up for the Robin Becker Poetry Prize and is forthcoming from Seven Kitchens Press. She was awarded the Galway Kinnell Scholarship to attend the Squaw Valley Community of Writers. Her poetry has appeared in literary journals such as *American Literary Review, Menacing Hedge, Labletter,* and others.

Steve Davenport is the author of two poetry collections: *Overpass* (2012) and *Uncontainable Noise* (2006). He's received a 2011 *Pushcart Prize* Special Mention in Fiction and a Notable listing in *Best American Essays* 2007. His website is http://gasolinelake.com/ .

Stephen Dunn is the author of 17 collections of poetry, including the recent *Lines of Defense* (Norton, 2013). His *Different Hours* was awarded the Pulitzer Prize. Among his many other awards are The Paterson Prize for Sustained Literary Achievement and an Academy Award in Literature from the American Academy of Arts & Letters. He lives in Frostburg, Maryland.

Greg Herriges's fiction and nonfiction works have appeared in The *Chicago Tribune* Magazine, *OUI, Story Quarterly, The Encyclopedia of Beat Literature, The Literary Review,* The *South Carolina Review*, and Great Britain's *Popular Music and Society* and *World Wide Writers*. He has published six novels, a collection of short stories, and a memoir about his meeting with legendary author J.D. Salinger. Herriges has twice won Aurora Awards for documentary screenwriting and producing, (*TC Boyle: The Art of the Story, Player: A Rock and Roll Dream*) and he was a credited guest on the BBC's television documentary *JD Salinger Doesn't Want to Talk. Flashback,* an album of his songs with the group Athanor, was released world-wide by Guerssen Records in 2013, and will be followed by a second album, *Love Shining,* in 2014. He is currently a professor of English at William Rainey Harper College in Palatine, Illinois.

Mark Hillringhouse's poems, interviews, articles, essays, book reviews and translations have appeared in: the *American Poetry Review, American Poetry, Columbia, Hanging Loose, The Literary Review, the Little Magazine, New American Writing, the New Jersey Monthly,* the *New York Times Book Review,* and many others. He has twice been nominated for a Pushcart Prize and has won the Chester H. Jones National Poetry Competition, and three fellowships from the New Jersey State Council on the Arts. For a look at his photographic work, visit http://mhillringhouse.zenfolio.com.

H. L. Hix's most recent poetry collection is *As Much As, If Not More Than* (Etruscan Press, 2014). He lives in the mountain west with his partner, the poet Kate Northrop, and writes in a studio that was once a barn. His website is www.hlhix.com.

Laura McCullough's most recent books are *Rigger Death & Hoist Another, poems* (Black Lawrence Press, 2013), *Ripple & Snap*, micro-fiction/prose-poems about the aftermath of a public suicide (ELJ Press, 2013), *The Smashing House*, a short fiction chapbook (ELJ Press, 2013), and her edited anthology, *The Room & the World: Essays on the Poetry of Stephen Dunn* (Syracuse University Press, 2013). Her other books are *Panic* (winner of the Kinereth Gensler Award, Alice James Books, and a BOTYA finalist), *Speech Acts* (Black Lawrence Press), and *What Men Want* (XOXOX Press). Her first book of poetry, *The Dancing Bear,* was published by the now defunct Open Book Press. Her second edited anthology, *A Sense of Regard: Essays on Poetry and Race* is forthcoming in late 2014 from University of Georgia Press. Also in 2014, Emerge Literary Journal Press will publish *Shutters*Voices*Wind*, linked monologues in the voices of women from around the globe, as well as reprint her poetry chapbook, *Women & Other Hostages*. She is the editor of *Mead: the Magazine of Literature and Libations* and an editor at large for *TranStudies Magazine*.

Roisin McLean has published fiction (under various pen names) in *Perigee: Publication for the Arts, Fiction Week Literary Review, Serving House: A Journal of Literary Arts*, and *Pithead Chapel*. Her essays appear in two anthologies: *Winter Tales II: Women on the Art of Aging*, and *OH SANDY!* (an anthology, all profits of which support survivors of Hurricane Sandy). Her interviews with ex-pat author Thomas E. Kennedy have appeared in *The McNeese Review* and *Ecotone*. She has been nominated four times for the Pushcart Prize and was a semifinalist for The Katherine Anne Porter Prize in Fiction (*Nimrod*/Hardman). She has worked as Managing Editor for Macmillan Publishing Company and in various capacities at other publishing houses, both on staff and freelance.

Rick Mulkey is the author of four books and chapbooks including, *Toward Any Darkness, Bluefield Breakdown*, and *Before the Age of Reason*. Previous work has appeared in *Poet Lore, Shenandoah, The Literary Review, South Carolina Review, Poetry East, The Georgia Review* and *The Southern Poetry Anthology: Volumes I and III*. He currently directs and teaches in the low-residency MFA program at Converse College.

Elisabeth Murawski is the author of *Zorba's Daughter,* which won the 2010 May Swenson Poetry Award, *Moon and Mercury*, and two chapbooks. Hawthornden Fellow 2008. Publications include *The Literary Review, The Yale Review, The Alaska Quarterly Review, et al.* A native of Chicago, she currently resides in Alexandria, VA.

Minna Proctor is Editor of *The Literary Review* and author of *Do You Hear What I Hear?* She has written for *Bookforum, The New York Times Book Review, The Nation, American Scholar, Aperture*, and others. She has translated a number of books from Italian, including *Love In Vain*, the selected stories of Federigo Tozzi. She teaches Creative Writing at Fairleigh Dickinson University.

Victor Rangel-Ribeiro, the award-winning Indian novelist, was born in Goa in 1925 when it was still a Portuguese colony, but he counts English among one of his three mother tongues. After he migrated to Bombay in 1939, his short stories were first published in the late 1940s and early 50s in the British Indian press; more recently they have been featured in the *North American, Iowa*, and *Literary Reviews*, as well as in other publications. The New York Foundation for the Arts awarded him its fiction fellowship in 1991; seven years later, his first novel, *Tivolem*, earned him the Milkweed National Fiction Prize. *Booklist* picked *Tivolem* as "one of the twenty notable first novels" of 1997-98. Penguin's paperback edition was short-listed for India's prestigious Crossword Book Award, and remained on that nation's bestseller list for several months.

Jack Ridl has published five collections of poems, the most recent being *Losing Season* (CavanKerry Press) and *Practicing to Walk Like a Heron* (Wayne State University Press). In 1996 The Carnegie Foundation (CASE)\ named him Michigan Professor of the Year. He has also co-authored with Peter Schakel *Approaching Literature* (Bedford/St. Martin's). He and Schakel are co-editors of the anthology 250 Poems (Bedford/St. Martin's). More than eighty of his former students are now published authors.

R.A. Rycraft has published stories, essays, reviews, and interviews in a number of journals and anthologies, including *Perigee, PIF Magazine, VerbSap, The MacGuffin*, and *Calyx*. Her short story collection *You Know* was a finalist in the 2009 Poets and Writers West Coast/East Coast Exchange Contest, and her short story "Covenant" was recognized with a Special Mention in the 2010 Pushcart Prize anthology. Winner of the Eric Hoffer Best New Writing Editor's Choice Award for 2008 as well as a 2006 Million Writers Award Notable Story, Rycraft is Creative Nonfiction editor of *Serving House Journal*, an Associate Professor of English at Mt. San Jacinto College in Menifee, California, and chair of the English Department.

Per Šmidl lived for two years in Wagon 537 at Christiania, the source of material for his novel *Wagon 537 Christiania*. Then he moved to Paris, then California and when he got back to Denmark he wrote the bestseller "Chop Suey." Many years as a political dissident in Prague followed after the publication in Denmark of his book *Victim of Welfare* in 1995. The book challenged the role and freedom of the individual in the welfare state. His previous publications include the novel *Mathias Kraft* (1999) and the essay "Ytringsfrihed," which means "Freedom of Speech", 2006.

Susan Tekulve is the author of *In the Garden of Stone*, winner of the 2012 South Carolina First Novel Award and a 2013 SIBA "Okra Award." She has also published three short story collections: *Savage Pilgrims, Wash Day* and *My Mother's War Stories*. Her stories and essays have appeared in *Shenandoah, The Georgia Review, New Letters, Best New Writing 2007, The Indiana Review, Denver Quarterly, Puerto del Sol, Prairie Schooner, North Dakota Quarterly, Connecticut Review, Beloit Fiction Journal, Crab Orchard Review, and The Literary Review.* She has been awarded a Sewannee Writers' Conference Scholarship and a Bread Loaf Writers' Conference Scholarship. An Associate Professor of English, she teaches in the BFA and MFA in creative writing programs at Converse College.

Dan Turèll (1946-1993) published one hundred books in his short lifetime —of poetry, novels, and creative nonfiction and numerous CDs and DVDs as well. He was honored by Denmark by a square and a café being named after him and a postage stamp was issued in his commemoration. In 2008, Thomas E. Kennedy began translating Turèll's poetry to American and his translations have been published in many literary journals. In 2013, PlantSounds records issued an English-language album, with Kennedy reading his translations of Turèll to the music of Halfdan E, a Danish film composer who inter alia did the music to *Borgen*. An audio sample from the CD with the text of one poem is contained on http://servinghousejournal.com/TurellLastWalk.aspx along with a link for ordering the album.

Timmy Waldron received his MFA from Fairleigh Dickinson in 2013 where he was the winner of the 2012 Senior Graduate Assistantship, and served as the Assistant Editor of *The Literary Review*. His short-story collection *World Takes* was published by Word Riot Press in 2009. He is an editor of *Best New Writing* and his fiction has appeared in *The McNeese Review, Serving House Journal, Mud Luscious Press, Dogzplot, Necessary Fiction, Sententia, Monkeybicycle,* and *What's Your Exit?* Work is forthcoming in *Keyhole Magazine,* and *The Word Riot Reader.* He stole the title of the story in this collection from a song.

Acknowledgments

Renée Ashley: "On Infidelity" first appeared in her novel *Someplace Like This* (The Permanent Press, 2003).

Dennis F. Bormann: "Fishhawk" was previously published in *The Main Street Rag* literary quarterly in the Fall of 2010 (Volume 15.4)

Flower Conroy: "God Trace" was published by *Sunsets & Silencers*; "Astronaut Affair" appeared in *Saw Palm*; "Decapitation" was part of the Tupelo Press 30/30 challenge for the month of April 2013.

Steve Davenport: "Dear Punch," first published in *New Letters* 79.1; "True Confessions," first published in *The Literary Review* 51.4, then in *Overpass* (poems), Arsenic Lobster/Misty Publications, August 2012.

Stephen Dunn: "The Imagined" was originally published in *The New Yorker*, and was chosen for *The Best American Poetry 2012* (Scribners), and also appeared in his book *Here and Now* (Norton, 2011).

Greg Herriges: A version of "Forgetting John Keats" appeared in his short story collection, *The Bay at Marseilles*.

H.L. Hix: "Sex is turquoise." From *Incident Light*. Etruscan Press, 2009.

Thomas E. Kennedy: "That Night on the Farm" appeared originally in *Last Night My Bed a Boat of Whiskey Going Down* and will be reprinted in *Serving House Journal*.

Laura McCullough: "The Elisionist, " "Meniscus: as distinct from other planets," and "The Man with Large Hands" first published in *Speech Acts*; "Women and the Syntactical World" first published in the chapbook *Women and Other Hostages*.

Roisin McLean: A version of "Cleavage" was originally published online with minor modifications as "Fitted Blouse—Silk" in *Serving House: A Journal of Literary Arts*, Spring 2012 issue.

Elisabeth Murawski: "That's Life" originally appeared in a different version in the online *Blue Lyra Review,* Spring, 2013; "Maytime" originally appeared in *The Southern Review,* Autumn, 2009.

Minna Proctor: "A Mystic at Heart" originally appeared in *Guilt & Pleasure, Winter 2008.*

Victor Rangel-Ribeiro: "Singular Desire" first appeared in his novel *Tivolem.*

Jack Ridl: "A Week After"—permission of the author; "Instead of Planting Roses" from *Practicing to Walk Like a Heron,* Wayne State University Press, 2013; "She's Selling Their Bed" from *The Chariton Review,* Vol. 36, No. 2; "Sunday Sermons" from *Between,* Dawn Valley Press, 1996; "What Are You Supposed To Do" from *Practicing to Walk Like a Heron,* Wayne State University Press, 2013.

Susan Tekulve: "Cherokee" first appeared as a chapter in her novel *In the Garden of Stone* (Hub City Press, 2013).